IT'S NOT
ALL ABOUT
THE RENT

A TENANT'S GUIDE TO CRACKING THE COMMERCIAL REAL ESTATE LEASE CODE

SCOT GINSBURG

INDIE BOOKS
INTERNATIONAL

ISBN 13: 978-1-952233-95-1
Library of Congress Control Number: 2022901549

Book design by Steve Plummer, spbookdesign.com

INDIE BOOKS INTERNATIONAL, INC.®
2424 VISTA WAY, SUITE 316
OCEANSIDE, CA 92054
www.indiebooksintl.com

CONTENTS

WHY IT'S NOT ALL ABOUT THE RENT

WHAT IF YOU could hold in your hand something with the power to make your company tens of thousands—or even millions—of dollars? What if that same everyday item could also single-handedly *cost* your company the same amount of money?

You can and it could.

When you sign a commercial lease, you are holding the ability to deliver profits directly to your bottom line—or to drain it.

Commercial leases are a complex undertaking; trying to research and compare all the variables that go into the process of housing your company's operations is not easy. Leases are rarely a plug-and-play proposition. Sadly, it's not likely to be related to the core competency of your business, so entering the arena of commercial real estate can be confusing, over-whelming, and stressful, especially when you consider all the factors in play: total lease obligation, annual rent, operational and building needs, space planning and efficiency, logistics, employee recruiting and retention, employee productivity, and corporate image.

What Your Landlord Knows That You Don't

The stakes are high, and chances are better than good that you are entering the exercise at a distinct disadvantage. You're up against negotiating partners who are full-time professionals with heavyweight knowledge, experience, and resources. They know most tenants can be distracted when it comes to making commercial space arrangements and agreements. They benefit from the fact that most lessees are eager to just settle it and get back to primary business matters. For unfocused executives, it's a miscue that, at best, leaves money on the table and, at worst, siphons huge sums from company earnings, not to mention the human capital time component, operational inefficiencies, etc.

If you have a good, long-standing relationship with your landlord and you're renewing your lease, you may think you can now trade in on the trust and goodwill you've banked to maintain favorable, market rate terms. It's a common mis-conception. Your current lease rate may have already peaked above the market rate by the end of its term.

This is business—and it's your landlord's business to keep the property at or above market rates. They know that renewing tenants are their most profitable deals, bar none. (Experience indicates that in general, a landlord's break-even renewal rental rate is about 60 percent of market rate when compared to the rate negotiated by a new tenant for that same space.) They are keenly aware that most companies balk at the prospect of relocating. All too often, tenants in lease renewals pay higher rental rates and receive fewer economic concessions than tenants negotiating a new lease for vacant space.

What Astute Lessees Know

While it's certainly not rocket science nor is it an unsolvable mystery, negotiating for commercial real estate will test your resolve. You'll need a shrewd counterplan to excel at the game and avoid being outplayed, which means you'll need a little moxie, too. Barring extreme market conditions and dumb luck, victors are better prepared and primed with superior strategy. Stack the deck in your favor by building a team of expert advisors. Add in an element of surprise by allowing landlords to underestimate you—and the degree of your determination.

Leases are multi-million-dollar decisions. For most companies, real estate represents one of their top three fixed expense categories. Retain a tenant representative broker (called a *tenant rep broker*) with a proven track record who knows that "getting the real estate right" can be a make-or-break proposition for overall company success. They realize that they're putting clients' careers on the line with every transaction. Companies looking for space in today's markets need that extra edge of having a professional services team with access to a full range of timely information and data (along with tenant-focused ethics, negotiating skills, and problem-solving strategies) to drive the best results. Resist the impulse go it alone, you will be setting yourself up for a Pro-Am match with any landlord or listing broker who regularly negotiates commercial real estate leases, compared to a tenant who will typically negotiate a real estate contract once every three to ten years..

Understand why it's not just about the rent. There are myriad lease terms to consider, and each situation is unique because commercial spaces differ, tenant needs vary, and space footprints are atypical. Desired concessions are many and varied, from lease term to reduced rent, free rent, capital improvements, to funding, to moving allowances to building services—the list goes on and on. You'll need to expect numerous expenses you may not have initially anticipated, such as professional fees for architects and designers, new fixtures and furnishings, parking, moving and fit-up expenses, and building utilities or services above and beyond the monthly rate, not to mention proper space planning for your current and future needs. Consider everything on your list and decide if some of those line items might be put up for negotiation. If you don't ask, you don't get.

Why It's About Leverage

Commercial real estate rates are ostensibly about determining a fair price for space, or the "market rate." In reality, there is no such thing as *market*: real estate pricing is subject to dramatic swings, depending on perceived leverage. Now it's a matter of who has the better position. That's often determined largely by who has the best knowledge about the art of the deal and how to deploy tactics. Clarity counts. Preparing a complete précis (summary or abstract) outlining what you need, what you want, what you're willing to relinquish, and what you're able to spend will give you the focus and confidence you'll need as you set out to skillfully solve the Rubik's cube of your next lease.

You are about to sign a major contract that has significant financial and legal implications for your company. Regardless of market influences, it's always wise to consider the landmines that can undermine your efforts and diffuse your leverage.

The first is waiting too long to start any commercial real estate process, whether it's relocating, expanding, or even negotiating a lease renewal. The key is to start the real estate process, whether a renewal or relocation, in parallel paths (even if you'd rather not move) twelve to twenty-four months from your lease expiration date, depending on your square footage size and type of space needed.

The next landmine is prematurely alerting your current landlord that you have interest in renewing before you've engaged your tenant representative. You will tip your hand; now your landlord knows you desire to stay. Tipping your hand prior to following the parallel path method,

> **Avoid Landmines That Can Undermine Your Efforts And Diffuse Your Leverage**
>
> **DON'T** wait too long to start any commercial real estate process.
>
> **DO** Begin 12-24 months ahead.
>
> **DON'T** prematurely alert your landlord that you are interested in renewing.
>
> **DON'T** defer the assembly of a team who can provide invaluable professional advice and direction.

is, as they say in boxing, telegraphing the punch. Allow the process deployed by your tenant representative to naturally alert your landlord, which will happen as a byproduct of your shopping for new space by also evaluating renewing.

A third landmine is deferring the assembly of a team who can provide invaluable professional advice and direction; it will definitely hamper your information and cripple the potency of your position—not only in critical areas of market data, space identification, and term sheet negotiation, but also in space planning, design, construction, and real estate contract negotiations.

Researching data points for leverage must include defining your negotiating partners' positions as well as your own. You'll want to discover what individual needs and motivations impel them. There are a lot of factors to consider, such as building cash flow pro formas, future rental projections, valuating your landlord's financial position with its current building in terms of existing or future vacancy, loan structure, tenant improvement costs to rebuild the space, downtime for vacancy, and more. To discover a landlord's drivers is to gain insight into how pliant or intractable they are likely to be on various elements, allowing you to define their "push points," or areas of likely concession. Your expert advisors will be able to help research and analyze findings to turn information into insights.

RECAP LAP
Why It's Not All About The Rent

The complexity and uniqueness of each leasehold negotiation can hardly be overstated. It's a game and you can win. Here are the steps:

1. Grasp the implications of what your next lease can mean for your company: a positive outcome can contribute directly to your bottom line, but a less favorable result can drain it for years. Consider all the factors in play including total costs, operational efficiency, employee morale, and corporate image.

2. Broaden your perspective to see your position from a landlord's point of view, then seek to understand their general positions, including their break-even rent on a renewal as well as specific needs and motivations.

3. Build a team of expert advisors to help provide information, advice, direction, and to partner with you through the leasing process. Chief among these is a real estate broker who specializes in representing tenants; this is your quarterback to lead other members of your team.

4. Marshal your resources to research and analyze data, knowing that good information translates to great leverage. Use what you've learned to codify your position as well as the positions of your negotiating partners.

5. Coalesce the information you've gathered into an outline of your position that gives you clarity and direction,

including your leverage points and a cogent summary of the positions of both your current and prospective landlord. Proceed with confidence.

HOW TO LEVEL THE PLAYING FIELD

I f you're going to level up your leasing game, you need to offset the unfair advantage of just about every landlord out there. And when you're outmatched, it calls for your best gamesmanship.

Now, you can even up the odds in your favor, but it's going to take more than one face card—and cogent insight into your opponent's strategy. So, when you perform valid due diligence and create the right game plan, you may even draw out a bit of surprise: your position—and your confidence—will reveal that you're not easy prey.

This inequality of starting positions is natural and expected. After all, it's a full-time occupation for most commercial landlords; they have more experience, better resources, and greater ability to focus on deals. Chances are good that, day to day, they practically hover in the weeds of lease terms and contracts, whereas tenants jump in intermittently, perhaps once every three, five, or ten years.

Engaging Your Team

To achieve the highest and best outcome for your company, you're going to need to *recruit a strong team*. Start with the most important partner you can have shoulder to shoulder

To achieve the highest and best outcome for your company, you're going to need to recruit a strong team.

with you: a tenant rep broker. That means someone (including the real estate brokerage firm) who doesn't represent landlords in any aspect, because that can create myriad conflicts of interest. Real estate firms who represent both landlords and tenants derive approximately 70 percent of their revenue from one type of client—the landlord, whereas tenant representation firms derive 100% of their revenue from one client type—the tenant.

Assuming you hired a tenant representation brokerage firm ensuring interests are aligned and landlord conflicts are avoided, it is equally important that your tenant representation firm also have a vertically integrated platform to be truly full service to the tenant's needs.This in-house integrated model should consist of domain experts in each area of the entire real estate project process:

- Real estate brokers (not real estate salespeople)

- Space planning and design professionals

- Workplace strategy experts

- Culture consulting

- Project and construction managers

- Real estate attorneys

- Portfolio lease administration, operating expense recovery, and lease audit services

This turnkey tenant model makes the process simpler and more robust, allowing you control over the entire journey with one integrated team. They will have the knowledge, resources, and experience to support you in gathering the information required for a well-considered leasing program. With a great brain trust behind you, you'll be able to approach your lease negotiation well prepared and ready with alternatives. Or as an early American settler might say, "Going in loaded for bear."

Cracking The Code

Most lessees neglect the critical elements of *preparation* that can provide a winning edge and deliver desired success later in the lease negotiation phase. Your willingness to delve into how the system works is an overwhelming advantage. Just knowing what you need to find out will lead you to uncover the data that will form the foundation of your proposition. Your team of trusted advisors will help you discover important trends and information about commercial real estate markets and *microclimates*, landlords' financials, leasing and operational objectives, customized space planning, construction costs, and unexpected or hidden expenses.

Research (including touring properties with your tenant rep broker) will provide you with a sound take on the markets. It will give you perspective and the information you'll need to understand your microclimate. Consideration of multiple options allows you to explore possibilities you may not have even been aware of. With timely due diligence, you'll be assured up front of prospective landlords' solvency and stability.

Great leverage begins with *clarity*. A well-considered outline of what your company needs and wants will serve as your true north through the process. Insight into motivations of landlords with whom you'll be negotiating will guide your understanding of their respective positions, helping you find the edge you'll need when you counter their terms. You'll know what concessions and considerations are important to you beyond the lease rate—and what unforeseen outlays may be lurking in each deal.

Examining Expenditures

A new lease, even a renewal, is a chance to reexamine your workplace for the efficiency of operations. This generally calls for tenant improvements, which is one of the most common leasehold concessions. An *existing conditions and needs assessment* (allowing for expansion or contraction per the business plan over the new lease term) will serve as the foundation of your *architectural program*. Retaining an architect or designer early on will help you define space needs and budgets required, whether you are reconfiguring existing space or building a new one. A preliminary space plan is important during the site selection process, regardless if it's a renewal or relocation, so you can refine estimated expenses and ensure a good fit for your operations. It's the no surprises approach to comparing alternatives.

It is important to do a needs assessment regarding whether you want to stay or leave. Let's say you are in 20,000 square feet and a needs assessment reveals that you only need 17,000 square feet. Well, each building is different. You would evaluate 17,000-square-foot spaces to move into, but this also helps if you are to renew. When you are looking at and negotiating 17,000-square-foot sites, it shows the landlord that you don't need all the 20,000 square feet you have now. Your needs assessment plan shows the landlord that you did your homework. Now the landlord knows he needs to either lower his square footage or lower the rent to make it comparable to a 17,000-square-foot space.

Forecasting and *financing* tenant improvement construction and outfitting costs can be tricky, too. Whether you are negotiating with a landlord to underwrite and provide all of the tenant improvement costs, self-funding all of the tenant improvement costs, or a combination of both, there are multiple financing alternatives and accounting implications. Find out what will work best for your company, in your individualized circumstances. For most small-to-midsized companies that have nonspecialized facilities, landlords will typically cover all improvement costs for the tenant. It is built into their rental rate. Larger companies or companies with specialized facilities that have capital to spend commonly weigh the pros and cons of different forms of financing the improvements.

You're going to want to cover your bases to *sidestep expensive missteps*. Be sure to forecast what kinds of major costs may be possible, depending on your lease type. For example, you may want to:

- Conduct an HVAC and roof audit.

- Ensure all utilities will meet your needs including power, water, back-up generators, and other specialized needs depending on your type of tenancy, such as office, biotechnology, R&D (research and development), GMP (good manufacturing practice) and other manufacturing, warehouse or distribution.

- Double-check code compliance and understand who is responsible to bring non-compliance items up to current codes.

- Confirm building feed data connectivity and internal IT needs including any supplemental HVAC.

- Assess parking needs and ensure there is sufficient parking for employees, parking for customers (if applicable) and some additional "flex" spaces for visitors or additional employees (and customers).

- Develop your exit strategy in case of early termination.

Your attorney, preferably one specializing in real estate in partnership with your tenant representation broker, will be able to offer a keen eye on lease terms that may be missing or overlooked. They can help you anticipate and provide for myriad smaller, but potentially costly line items such as fixed versus floating lease start date, tenant improvement cost overruns, after-hours HVAC, signage, holdover rent, and more. Consulting an expert who's got your six on technicalities can be invaluable.

Where We Are Headed

By now, you should have a basic understanding of why it's important to level up your game. This chapter outlines the steps you'll need to take to get to a promising final contract. It's intended as an introduction to all the things you'll need to consider at the outset, as well as an overview of more detailed content ahead.

Next, we'll break down the considerations you'll need to tackle from start to finish, how to plan and prepare for leasing success, what you'll need to do to ensure a continued advantage, and how to plan for workplace changes in your company's future. You might just conclude it's best to stay on top of your game by monitoring the market and watching the players. When the timing is right, you can then jump back in with the whip hand.

Walking A Mile

The reason I can offer insight into this process is because I've been there, done that. I have well over twenty years' experience as a commercial real estate broker, exclusively representing tenants in lease and purchase negotiations. I've learned a lot about how landlords think, how they size up tenants, how to discern what's motivating them, and how to negotiate deals on par with them.

Yet, the true value I bring to clients is that I've walked a proverbial mile in those moccasins. I was a passionate dot com entrepreneur in the 1990s and cofounder of an online technology company. The agent I hired to secure our office space worked for a commercial real estate firm who represented both tenants and landlords. Having grown up in a family with a few modest commercial holdings in the Santa Monica area of Los Angeles, I thought I knew a bit about commercial real estate. Real estate was in my blood; it was small talk around the dinner table. As a teenager, I learned a lot about my family's real estate holdings.

After college, I started my own business and it seemed natural that I would handle the leasing process to secure my first office space. It was soon painfully clear to me that I was on an uneven, conflicted playing field during the entire negotiation process. Against my better judgment but feeling confident in the success of my venture, I agreed to a personal guarantee under my name as a condition of the contract.

The sad, short story is that the landlord pulled a bait-and-switch routine on me. When my business went south, I had to pay a large sum of money to negotiate a lease termination.

I lost nearly everything. Clearly, my broker hadn't protected me from this possibility in my contract. Sadly, his firm held *dual agency*, meaning the same broker (or members of the same brokerage firm) represented both the buyer and the seller in the transaction. I felt taken and embarrassed, believing I should have somehow known better.

Devastated, I clearly learned through experience that the tenant was the underdog in lease transactions. I wanted to level this playing field. When I made the career change to commercial real estate, I knew the only way to go was to work exclusively for tenants, the end consumer. My righteous indignation fueled a passion for serving clients at the highest level of my ability. I knew my focus had to be on ensuring that none of my client companies would be subjected to a compromised position.

After several early years of cutting my teeth and struggling to learn the ropes in a small commercial real estate business that exclusively served tenants, I finally landed a position with a national tenant representation firm, a position I held for nine years. That 1,200-person firm earned zero dollars from landlords and did not manage or own buildings, allowing us freedom from ethical conflicts. When a full-service firm purchased that company, things slowly changed over the remaining four-year period of my tenure.

As I had never worked at such a firm,

How could I tell people that we represented a tenant's best interest when only a small portion of revenue was actually derived from the tenant's side of the business?

I was not 100 percent sure conflicts of loyalty even arose at full-service firms, though after four years, I witnessed several apparent conflicts a day—day in and day out. The tenant representation model I had worked so long to establish is not a recurring revenue model—I depended on my reputation for referrals and repeat business; it was my goal to build a clientele for life.

Trying to represent my clients' best interests became increasingly difficult, since full-service firms (representing tenants and landlords) derive about 70 percent of their revenue from landlord listings (leasing, selling, and buying buildings for landlords). These firms also own a lot of real estate which makes them even more conflicted. Now, how could I tell people that we represented a tenant's best interest when only a small portion of the firm's revenue was actually derived from the tenant's side of the business? It was not the core focus of the firm.

So, I decided to join an exclusive tenant representation only firm to once again be free from such dilemmas. It's been fantastic to be able to bring clarity and balance to the equation in the tenant-landlord matchup. Over the past two decades, I have helped nearly 2,000 clients with all of their commercial real estate needs. It's hard work and totally customized because no two companies and no two leasing opportunities are the same. Maybe that is what makes it so deeply satisfying, as it was recently, when I put together a complex leasing arrangement that will save my client several hundreds of thousands of dollars, to even millions of dollars, over their lease term.

Taking the time to fully understand each company's unique situation is just one of the reasons clients continue to work with me and refer business to me. I am known as a tech and a car guy who is always learning something new, so I am well suited to a field that is always changing. I have a passion for helping people and have extensive knowledge of the technical details of facility infrastructures, real estate financing, venture funding, burn rates, and lease contracts. You could say I have become a master at lease puzzle solving.

It's my joy to share with you the insight I've unlocked through years of hard-wrought experience and to fulfill my mission of bringing a bit of illumination to the commercial lease game. I guide hard-working executives who seek equity and fairness on the field of commercial real estate.

RECAP LAP
How To Level The Playing Field

By following a few steps to research, develop, and negotiate your well-considered position, you'll be amazed at the success you can achieve in creating great terms for your next lease:

1. Concede how easy it is to be outplayed in the leasing game, and decide you're going to delve into learning what it takes to prevail. Know that you're already ahead just by understanding this and being willing to learn what it will take.

2. Recruit a strong team to provide information, advice, and guidance—a tenant representation broker, project and construction manager, space planner, architect, general contractor, real estate attorney, and other specialty consultants—as needed. High stakes commercial leasing is a team sport.

3. Compile extensive research to determine critical success factors. This may include an assessment of your company's true needs, market data analysis and trends, landlords' motivations and financials, space planning, and budget forecasting and financing.

4. Heighten your awareness about common leasehold and contractual missteps and blind spots. Consult your team when negotiating and reviewing lease terms and benefit from their experience.

5. Avoid the costly and demoralizing mistakes I made as a young entrepreneur by surrounding yourself with dedicated and experienced people who will guide you in best practices. Quarterback their efforts to orchestrate a strategy that will advance your operations and deliver high value on this investment in your company.

ASSESS YOUR SPACE NEEDS

T HE PATH OF least resistance might be an expensive
road.

So, the time and attention you invest in mapping
an ideal course could yield big savings. To avoid leaving
money on the table, you will want to sidestep the ready–fire–
aim approach. Is it in your best interest to renew or to renegotiate your current lease, and if so, should you be paying
market rent or below market as a repeat customer? Is it truly
clear that you need to relocate, expand, or add another location? OK, then where and why?

It literally pays to thoughtfully consider your future space
needs and thoroughly analyze your options. Thinking through
your near-future infrastructure requirements might indicate
space expansion, contraction, or reconfiguration. Good up-front

space planning and a proper needs assessment will provide confidence that you are heading in the right direction, be it renewing or renegotiating your lease, or moving to a new location.

Renewing Your Lease: Get An Early Start

Over the years, I have learned that approximately 70 percent of all tenants renew or extend their real estate lease. Landlords know this fact and it's the reason why most tenants pay market rent versus paying below-market rent when renewing. In addition, most tenants end up expanding, contracting, or restructuring their lease well in advance of the lease expiration. Did you know that lease renewals are a landlord's highest profit deal, in most cases, by a huge margin? Before you just pick up the phone and tell your landlord you're ready to renew, think about the Pro-Am analogy previously mentioned. Make sure you underwrite the landlord's break-even point and work with your tenant broker. Do you really think the landlord is not going to get market intel and consult with their listing brokers, real estate lawyers, and construction team to arm them the best way possible before negotiating with you? Why make this a Pro-Am match?

And if you think you will save the commissions, think again, because someone *always* gets paid; no one works for free. If you go direct, most likely your landlord will pay themselves a commission as an in-house leasing broker, or they will pay their listing broker the commission for both the landlord and the tenant listing sides, since technically, there is only one broker: the landlord if you go direct or their listing agent who is acting as a *dual agent*.

There is a leverage maximization window that increases your bargaining power and then starts to slowly close when the lease expiration date is near enough that your landlord knows you cannot move. Make sure you do not miss this window and know how to exercise the leverage you have to drive the best deal. The leverage maximization window varies with the size of your space. While a 5,000-square-foot tenant may need ten months to follow the proper renewal/relocation process, a 100,000-square-foot tenant will need to start up to thirty-six months in advance of the lease expiration. Also, biotech and companies with heavy infrastructure require much longer lead times to create maximum buying power in any market.

Understanding the needs and motivations of your landlord is key to assessing if and when you should initiate an early renewal. For example, owners who are looking at refinancing or selling the property can be very motivated to obtain newly signed leases that reflect a longer-term income stream. Is your current or future landlord a buyer and flipper? Then their motivation is likely to attain a high rent to ensure the real estate value is the greatest. Is it likely that this landlord will consider granting you an abundance of free rent or other concessions? This landlord may be willing to consider capital improvements that will increase (significantly) the market value of the property.

Or perhaps your current or future landlord is a REIT (real estate investment trust). or other cash-driven landlord such as a small mom-and-pop business, and they care a lot about occupancy and cash flow, which often results in lower rent with a smaller concession package than a value-add (buyer/flipper) landlord. It's imperative to keep your ear to the ground on what is happening with your landlord as well as with the surrounding market and competing landlords, especially if you're within two years of the end of your lease. Just remember, while most tenants negotiate a commercial real estate lease once every three, five, or seven years, landlords do this every day. Just as you are shopping for the best building and landlord, landlords are shopping for the best tenant.

Blend And Extend

A key strategy in renegotiating commercial real estate leases is the *blend and extend* approach, whereby you trade an early lease renewal and extended lease duration for better terms. Depending on your objectives, these may include reduced rent, capital improvements, and contracted or expanded leasehold footprint. The blend and extend approach trend is more common when market rents are falling and tenants are paying higher than market rents.

When you're currently paying above the market rate, you've got great leverage to drive your rate down to market, or even below market, by negotiating an early renewal. This also can be combined with concessions such as early free rent or early tenant improvement allowances. If there is potential for rates to climb by the end of your current lease, an early renewal can lock in your rate, which could result in appreciable savings over the term of a new lease.

If your growth plans call for expanded or contracted space, leveraging an early lease renewal can be a great way to get landlord concessions; possibly a lower rate on the new space, enhanced tenant improvement allowances, or even advancing your ability to shed square footage you are not using. Adding space with an early lease renewal offers you an edge because the landlord is getting the double benefit of an extended lease and additional leased-out space.

Downsizing can be a little trickier because you don't have quite as much leverage. When you are asking the landlord to take space back in exchange for extending the lease term, there is no up-front benefit to the landlord. But it's important to look at the big picture and not fixate on the lease rate alone. By modeling the aggregate costs of carrying less space now through the new lease term, you can often find significant total savings through early renewal.

Reconfiguring existing space can be very expensive and often hard to negotiate close to lease expiration. If you require remodeling and construction to meet changing business operations, an early lease renewal puts you in the best position to negotiate an early tenant improvement allowance from your landlord. Just make sure you don't spend a lot of capital in your space (remodeling, etc.) when you have less than 50 percent of the term remaining. Otherwise you're hinting to the landlord there's no way you're going to move.

Renegotiating Your Lease: Accelerate Your Understanding

Remember the concept called buyer loyalty? Faithful to a brand, you're a repeat customer for a number of years and typically get a discount or reward. Makes sense, right? However, that's not really the way it works in commercial real estate.

Most leases provide for rent increases each and every year, so that even if the starting rent was reasonable, it may end up being above market by the end of the term.

Most often, tenants who renew their existing lease pay higher rental rates and receive fewer economic concessions than tenants negotiating a new lease for vacant space. Does this mean that a landlord will give better terms to a new, untested company than to a loyal, repeat customer? Typically, yes, unless you know how to navigate the hazards and maximize your negotiating leverage. The bottom line: a landlord's cost to find a new tenant is typically four to five times higher than a tenant's cost to move to a new building.

Don't discount the leverage you have on a renewal. Regrettably, this leverage normally comes at the eleventh hour—when the fear of relocation is real; your landlord will always want a last bite at the apple provided you exercise the market and landlords competing for your tenancy. Competing landlords are hungry to earn new tenants, simply because most often they are sitting on vacant space and need to fill the holes. A landlord with a renewing tenant takes some pushing since they have not hit a gap in their income, therefore not yet trying to plug a hole in revenue.

Renegotiating a lease requires a set strategy that involves research, preparation, and bargaining. Remember, a lease renewal is often the landlord's best play

Most leases provide for rent increases each and every year, so that even if the starting rent was reasonable, it may end up being above market by the end of the term.

because it's the most profitable deal. Know your position and learn as much as you can about your landlord's starting line.

A little insider information to clarify the landlord's point of view can be helpful here. A landlord who keeps an existing tenant—rather than letting the space go vacant and spending money to secure a new tenant—dodges rental income downtime, saves on tenant improvement costs to remodel for a new tenant, avoids risk with a new tenant, and keeps their occupancy stabilized. All of which leads to higher profits because over time, the landlord's breakeven on renewal rent is estimated to be about 60 percent of the prevailing market rent. When a relationship of trust and mutual respect has already been established, your landlord should also relax requirements for the security deposit and/or a letter of credit (LOC).

Lease renewal negotiations are ostensibly about determining a fair price for space, or the *market rate*. In reality, there is no such thing as *market*, and real estate pricing is subject to dramatic swings depending on real or perceived bargaining position. Some tenants engage a real estate brokerage firm when they plan to relocate their business, but not when renewing their office lease. Think about what message this sends to the landlord: *I am staying put*. You have just telegraphed your first punch. Since the landlord knows the chance of your relocating is low, they will push on their rent agenda much stronger, and also might slow play the negotiations, thereby making it even more difficult to relocate by running down your clock.

What is the first thing you'd do if you were set on moving? Hire a good tenant representation broker to kick off the process to address space needs and locate sites for the executive team to tour. Treating the renewal the same as if you were, in fact, moving, is the most important point and key influencer in a successful renewal.

If your landlord calls you and tells you not to use a broker, alarm bells should be going off. Would you sell your business without any advisors? Of course not. This seldom happens, but if it does, beware. They may say they won't have to pay a commission if you renew directly with them. Not the case. Remember, the landlord will pay themselves or their in-house leasing agent, or their broker who you didn't even know is getting paid. A good broker should be saving their tenant client many times over the commission or fee they earn.

Treating the renewal, especially the negotiation timeline, as if you were moving is the most important point and key influencer in a successful renewal.

When a business is faced with unforeseen and unexpected challenges, the blend and extend strategy can offer true redemption. Once a biotech company pioneering agricultural technology experienced a delayed funding round. Negotiating a lease extension while in a difficult financial situation significantly impaired leverage with their landlord and eliminated the chance to create credible leverage through relocation. With a blend and extend approach, I renegotiated their lease two years prior to the expiration date, quickly providing early concessions such as free rent and bringing them current on their lease obligation. The recast terms also saved the company $1 million, which was realized in just twelve months.

Relocation: Get A Rolling Start

Whether your company is a start-up, or you've decided you need to relocate, there are a number of factors to consider in developing your plan. Location, for example, is just one of the things that should guide your decision. There's also quality, rental rate, security deposit, tenant improvements, maintenance, infrastructure, furniture, and current and future space needs.

How much space should your company lease? That's the million-dollar question. Before you start touring space with your real estate partner, take some time to map out headcount projections and conduct the necessary space assessments. Some type of headcount plan is better than none, since you can match these growth rates with expansion rights in the lease and/or in the term length of the lease.

Many organizations have a difficult time projecting their headcount three to five years in advance. Yes, it's hard to see that far into the future, but give it your best shot. Extract forecasts from the business plan that correlate to headcount for each year and calculate five years out. If five years is too long, try three years. Use general rules of thumb to narrow in on the number of square feet required per person to account for total space needs for each year. (As good place to start, general office tenants typically require 200 square feet per person; biotechnology and R&D companies need roughly 300 square feet per person, due to the lighter density in the laboratory areas.) Then figure out specialty areas, departments of growth, adjacencies, and use type. Far too many companies ballpark their space needs and find themselves with too much or too little space in the early stage of their lease.

Tenants in mid-lease term who find themselves out of space are sometimes in a real predicament. Provided the current landlord has adjacent space available, it's an easy fix. However, it's very likely the rate per square foot will increase, given the landlord has a captive audience and knows you are more likely to pay a little higher rate for convenience. Depending on the existing furniture layout, reconfiguring workstations, doubling up people in private offices may be a faster, easier, and less expensive solution. However, when considering how long you can live with doubling up in offices combined with forecasted market conditions, you might be better off to lease extra space early as a Band-Aid, or even take another space but gradually phase in the rent over time to help ease payments on two spaces.

Most security deposits for sublease space are a fraction of what landlords will require compared to leasing direct space from a building owner.

While subleasing space may not seem glamorous (thanks, in part to the *as-is* condition of the facility), you can find great value as the second owner. Most companies who are downsizing or marketing space for sublease are in loss mitigation mode and more motivated to grant concessions than building owners are. It's usually possible to negotiate about a 30 percent rate reduction (pending market conditions), in addition to more free rent on subleases, than leasing direct space from a landlord. That's a huge savings. Many times, start-ups can obtain included assets such as phone systems and furniture, which can be a massive benefit.

The biggest benefit to subleasing, however, can be the security deposit for start-up businesses or those in the red. Most security deposits for sublease space are a fraction of what landlords will require compared to leasing direct space from a building owner. And if you're on a shoestring budget, that's key.

Landlords would love nothing more than to rent additional space to their tenants. Tenants suddenly become a captive audience with little or no negotiating power. In this case, the landlord may be reluctant to line up the expiration dates. Make sure the expansion space expires the same day as the existing lease. Otherwise, it can be a quagmire when a relocation or renewal occurs, since dealing with two different lease expirations hinders a tenant's free agency.

"We negotiated an expansion right when we moved in and now that we need the space, our right is void." Sound familiar? Many landlords hate giving certain expansion rights, so if you were astute enough to obtain an expansion right it was most likely a *right of first offer* (ROFO). These rights can burn off quickly. Next time, negotiate a *right of first refusal* (ROFR). The landlord must fully negotiate a deal with a third party and then give you first shot at the space whereby you must match that third-party offer. This ROFR is more likely to be valid for a longer period of time within the lease term.

For most businesses, real estate represents one of the top three expense categories (along with payroll), and most leases are multi-million-dollar decisions. As you suit up to compete as an outsider in the world of commercial real estate, equip yourself with the best information available: define your company's needs and wish list, understand the market, research the landlord or building owner's position and motivation, and explore alternative options. The bottom line will always be results, because *getting the real estate right* is a significant contributor to company success.

RECAP LAP
Assess Your Needs

Let's review the steps to map your best course:

1. Consult your business plan and conduct a needs analysis and space plan to determine your company's requirements three to five years out. Decide if your business plan supports maintaining, expanding, contracting, or reconfiguring your existing space.

2. Research and compare your current lease rate with current and projected market rates. If you prefer to stay in your location, investigate your landlord's situation and motivations, then conduct competitive research to leverage your position. For a maximum edge, start the renewal or relocation process well ahead of the end of your lease term—which can be as much as thirty-six months. But most tenants should start the process or plan a strategy eighteen to twenty-four months from lease expiration. Plus, it is almost always a dual path— you want to start the renewal or relocation process at the same time.

3. Initiate the real estate process with your due diligence in hand, having determined if renewing, renegotiating early, or relocating is your best play. Just make sure to follow the same timeline for a renewal as a relocation. Prioritize your objectives among rent, tenant improvements, capital improvements, flexibility with your business plan, and expanded or contracted leasehold term.

4. Factor several criteria when considering a relocation: location, quality, rental rate, security deposit, tenant improvements, maintenance, infrastructure including parking spaces, furniture, size, and the type of the landlord. Compute headcount projections for the years covered by a new lease term and determine square feet per person. Add in specialty areas, departments of growth and type to determine how much space you'll need.

5. Evaluate subleasing alternatives, which can sometimes offer better value and savings, as well as reduced security deposit requirements. Appraise the value and simplicity that plug-and-play alternatives may offer.

6. Match up lease expiration timelines when adding expansion space to an existing leasehold. Negotiate a *first right of refusal* with your landlord so you have a legitimate crack at newly available space at your location.

7. Monitor your company's evolving space needs, stay abreast of market conditions, follow your landlord's business, and explore options to capitalize on opportunities for cost efficiency to your company's bottom line.

RESEARCH MARKET RELOCATION OPTIONS (INCLUDING A LEASE RENEWAL)

WHEN IT COMES to your commercial real estate position, do you know what you need to know? Do you know what you don't know? Do you know how to find out?

Chances are, you're already a pretty good investigator if you conduct due diligence as a matter of business. Before signing a big contract, you conduct background and credit checks on potential employees and business partners, right? You probably track what's going on in your industry and follow regional, national, and economic trends that could affect your business.

Gleaning good intel on real estate market trends, coupled with knowing how to uncover and leverage a landlord's needs to your best advantage can be a real game-changer that's worth the legwork. Whether you are getting toward the end of an existing lease term and considering renewal or you're looking for new space, it's always a good idea to discover the motivations of potential landlords. It's also important to realize that the objectives of landlords and their lenders are not always aligned; they're often subject to the changing dynamics of macroeconomic forces.

For example, during the commercial real estate peak from 2006 to 2007, it was mostly all about rates for landlords. Every five cents per square foot per month for a 10,000-square-foot block of space increases or decreases the valuation of that 10,000-square-foot block of real estate by nearly $100,000. Just a small example of how important five cents per square foot per month is to a landlord.

It's no different with the value of your company, which is likely to be calculated on total sales and revenue. Back then, the rate trend line was strongly upward, so property owners were less concerned about vacancy rates and more focused on maximizing lease rates. At that time, lenders and potential buyers were confident that rates would continue to rise. Vacancy levels were not as important to them. Then, we all know what happened to the economy in the recession of 2008.

Today, most landlords are intent on maintaining occupancy levels with more rate flexibility with the exception of real estate for biotech companies, industrial real estate, and areas where big tech gobbles up all the office space, currently at an all-time high throughout the United States. Landlords seek to eliminate vacancies and drive up their overall capitalized lease assets. Potential tenants who know this have the best opportunities to gain major concessions in exchange for inking a multi-year lease.

If your current office lease is expiring within twelve to twenty-four months, you are paying above-market rent, and your creditworthiness is strong, you may be able to negotiate an early rate reduction of 25 to 30 percent. First, however, it's wise to research and weigh multiple factors to strike a deal that works both in the short-term and over the long run—and protects you from potential landlord insolvency.

From a big picture perspective, occupancy levels have become more important. Any building full of tenants with multi-year leases is much more saleable than one with a lot of potential but also a lot of vacancies. In addition, landlords looking to refinance their properties are in a stronger position when they can show a solid portfolio of multi-year lease assets.

Understand leasing microclimates in each submarket to get the best fit for your needs and drive the best deal.

Examining Market Conditions And Microclimates

We have all learned that regional weather forecasts can be useless when talking about the *microclimate* of your own neighborhood. A "mostly sunny" weekend forecast doesn't mean much when a storm rains out your kid's soccer game.

The same analogy applies in the commercial real estate market. Regional lease rates and occupancy trends provide a useful backdrop, however, it's vital to understand *leasing microclimates* in each submarket to get the best fit for your needs and drive the best deal for your budget. It's not just geography, either: what's happening to the market in the bio-tech, industrial, R&D, and GMP manufacturing sectors has a unique affect on nearly all commercial real estate.

In general, if your office space needs are in the 3,000 to 10,000-square-foot range, there are many options to consider in each microclimate. However, when your space requirements are in the 40,000-square-foot range on up, options become limited. There might be only one or two alternatives for a large tenant in each submarket. A big tenant is at risk of influencing these microclimates as they search for space; brokers begin to speculate on that tenant's available options. Ultimately, a larger tenant might require a *build to suit* space for their special needs, which is most often the case for large biotech companies or those requiring a large headquarter location, which can open up more options. Note: A build to suit space can take about twenty-four months to construct and be move-in ready from the time the lease is signed. This is about a three-year project in total.

To drive the best deal, tenants need to formulate their search strategy more carefully than ever, rather than just touring the region without a deliberate approach. Tenants may hurt their negotiating leverage or even inflate the entire market when they put out proposals to buildings that are not strongly in consideration because it creates a false sense of demand. To be sure, most landlords can sense this lack of sincere interest; it is their profession and their livelihood. No landlord wants to be approached by a stalking horse, so if that strategy comes into play to drive the best deal for you, make sure you have an excellent jockey in the saddle on your side.

If a landlord only has one viable tenant to consider, they have to get aggressive in making that one deal work. Yet, if a broker without a set strategy has fielded six RFPs (request for proposals) to landlords for their tenant client, now there are six landlords out there with unknown hopes of being the winning bidder. The more a landlord senses they can secure your tenancy—provided you have a proper strategy in place and then execute it—the more they will stretch to make your deal. Oftentimes the better target you give a landlod to hit the better the chance of a winning solution or outcome.

Although market opportunities for larger tenants may be more limited, there are still techniques you can use to uncover better alternatives. If viable, consider expanding the search into areas beyond just your preferred microclimate. Another approach is to split operations into multiple locations. This is particularly apt if you have a mixed-use space containing office, warehouse, manufacturing, biotech, R&D etc., if the warehouse, biotech, or non-office portion limits your choices in the market. It's also the only option when one building is unable to fully house operations, as with large companies requiring from 100,000 to millions of square feet. While splitting space may initially seem less desirable, by developing those options in parallel, you may bolster your negotiating position with potential landlords—and provide better operational solutions than you may have otherwise envisioned.

Strive to understand what is happening within your industry and follow vacancy rates in your specific microclimate. For example, when laboratory space vacancies are at a record high, prices can drop significantly as slumping biotech firms leave a trail of vacant lab space behind. Soaring vacancy rates in specialty sectors can slash rental rates one-third or more from their market peak. It's worth keeping an eye on industry-specific as well as general commercial vacancy trends.

Here is one caveat for all office and industrial tenants, especially the biotech industry, when considering a move or any type of tenant improvements (even a remodel of your current space): If you decide to renew, be sure to lock in pricing on a space plan with the customized improvements you require. One small mistake in the construction process may offset any savings you garner, so work closely with your real estate advisor and project manager to ensure a realistic project budget is firmly in place. In biotech, for instance, there are specialized components that need to be well understood, such as power, piping, plumbing, fume hoods, clean rooms, tissue culture rooms, and HVAC capacity. Should the landlord be unable to fund your entire construction costs, make sure you know this well in advance of the negotiation process.

Heeding Signs Of The Times

With workplace shifts in 2020, landlords found themselves in a vastly different competitive environment with a tighter race to secure new tenants, compete with the increase in sublease space availability, and retain existing occupants. But as we all know, in many areas of the country the demand for not only industrial and biotech space is at an all time high, office space is also being absorbed faster than anticipated with the onramping of companies wanting to get back to the office. If your company has a lease expiring in the next twelve to twenty-four months, rest assured, the chance your landlord wants to keep you is extremely high. If they call, listen closely; their knees may be knocking. The first shot over the bow from a landlord can tell a lot about their motives.

Suddenly, landlords with lower occupancy ratings in their portfolios no longer prefer to sit on vacant space and watch their property appreciate in value versus enjoying a stable income stream. It became all about cash flow, which for them, means tenants who pay rent. "What is it going to take to get this deal done?" quickly became the most commonly asked question in negotiations for office space. As homage to the *build it and they will come* theory, property owners were more willing to fill vacant space by outfitting new suites on a speculative basis (spec suites). Landlords also homed in on securing existing tenants far in advance of the lease expiration to forestall their lessees entering competitive markets with competitive landlords. On the opposite end of the spectrum, industrial and biotech landlords were building like crazy in 2020, speculating that tenants would come. Demand for that space type could not be delivered fast enough.

Here are two common signals that your landlord is nervous about their position:

Early Renewal: Landlords are actively working to fill their vacant space with new tenants while also becoming more proactive in retaining existing ones. If you have twelve to thirty months left on your lease term and you get a call to renew early, it could be a sign the landlord is fearful that the market is headed south or concerned about retaining you as a tenant, or maybe they want to refinance or sell your building, which could provide you with a lucrative opportunity. Typically, the bigger the space, the longer the lead time. The landlord's objective: eliminate future competition from other landlords who have vacant space. The aim is to get ahead of the curve and to preclude a tenant from investigating the market and discovering alternatives. A landlord does not want tenants shopping the market to find better economic alternatives that help drive down renewal rates (which is the exact reason why you should). If you are approached by your landlord to renew early and are not currently paying above-market rents, sit tight and enjoy your affordable space, provided the building meets your operational needs. Also, if we are in the beginning of a stock market bull run there might be an opportunity to lock in your lower rate early, hedging your bet, so to speak.

Spec Suites: As a rule of thumb, newly built or renovated yet unoccupied office suites in the 2,000 to 10,000-square-foot size range usually lease faster than do unimproved (shell) spaces for similar size ranges. Yet in a healthy market, landlords often prefer to leave new suites in shell condition so they can customize improvements and eliminate the risk of wasted tenant improvement dollars. This motivation evaporates when the market is soft, because many owners choose to improve shell suites on a speculative basis, hoping for shortening lease-up time. Plus, many small-space tenants prefer to skip the construction process and are more attracted to newly improved, move-in ready spaces.

With respect to market trends and temperature, remember that landlords are also closely watching for signs of a downturn or rebound. They are always adjusting their negotiating positions to take advantage of any pricing leverage that might result from an upward trend in demand. Landlords who are betting on the market improving may be reluctant to start lease renewals if those leases are still a couple of years from expiring. A proper negotiating strategy and real story of why an early negotiation is in the tenant's and landlord's best interest will oftentimes help reluctant landlords come around.

Realistically, there is never a clear "starting bell" to signal a rebound, and rarely is it an easily discernable, across-the-board upswing. When companies are slowly beginning to hire, it may take time for overall market demand to gain traction. In the meantime, companies that have flexibility with regard to space size, amenities, location, and the like have a great opportunity to target the soft spots in a shifting market. This is the optimal time to lock in an excellent long-term deal before the rebound hits full stride.

Steering Clear Of Red Flags

Not long ago, it was rare for a tenant to worry about the performance and stability of their landlord. Be cautious of smaller or less capitalized landlords who may not be able to weather a market downturn. Cabi Developers was one of the first institutional real estate investment groups to purchase a Southern California real estate portfolio from Arden Realty/General Electric Real Estate, now Blackstone, at the market peak's pre-2008 crisis only to hand the keys back to their equity partners

45

about eighteen months later. This debacle sent shock waves through the market, signaling the start of a downward spiral in regional commercial real estate. Corporate downsizing and a credit crisis made it impossible to achieve rental rate projections that once validated high purchase prices.

Now, more than ever, tenants must understand a landlord's ability to perform in accordance with the lease. Should the lender foreclose on the property, the tenant may be at risk in several ways. Does the lease stay intact, or will the lessee be kicked out? How will the free rent period and tenant improvement allowance be honored, if at all? Who maintains the building?

The list continues. While it is impossible to eliminate 100 percent of the risk should the landlord default, it is important for tenants to underwrite their business partner's financial stability before executing a lease. There are some safeguards that can guide your understanding about whether a landlord can fulfill their end of the agreement.

This research checklist can help you reduce your risk when leasing space:

Landlord Equity: Has the landlord's equity evaporated, with debt outweighing asset worth? This is a red flag unless the landlord has deep pockets to weather the storm. Discern the current value of the building, the owner's purchase price, and loan amount.

Debt Stacks: Institutional investors often cross-collateralize a loan on a single building with several buildings in their portfolios. This strategy helps lenders reduce their risk. If a property is cross-collateralized, you will want to learn how the landlord's entire portfolio is performing in order to accurately assess the risk. Should a single building in a portfolio be underperforming but the balance of the portfolio is solid, this situation could be far less risky than the inverse.

Cash Position: What's the landlord's cash position? While this is readily understood for a publicly traded REIT (real estate investment trust), it can be problematic when underwriting a private ownership of real property. However, most real estate professionals should have enough market intelligence to investigate this situation with private landlord entities and counsel you accordingly.

Subordination, Non-Disturbance and Attornment Agreement (SNDA): This agreement between the lender of the property and the tenant ensures that your lease remains intact in the event the lender takes possession of the building. It helps navigate challenging issues that could arise around the free rent period or tenant improvement allowance. Lenders often won't agree to assume those obligations even if they foreclose on the asset. Yet, there are other avenues your broker may pursue should the lender become intractable when negotiating this agreement.

Offset Rights: This lease clause is fairly standard in today's environment for creditworthy or large tenants. Should the landlord fail to perform, offset rights allow you to redirect rental payments to fund your own tenant improvements or as credit for other monies owed, such as free rent or repairs that a defaulting landlord is not able to honor.

Building Maintenance: A newer building or a building in stellar shape typically has a lower risk related to future issues around building maintenance and building systems needing replacement during your lease term. An older building or one that betrays deferred maintenance has a higher risk of future maintenance and building systems replacement issues. Building owners of older, maintenance-deferred properties who appear to be encountering financial difficulties are a huge liability for tenants—all the more reason to obtain offset rights in older, deferred-maintenance buildings.

Imagine this scenario: A tenant executes a lease but during the tenant improvement process, the landlord defaults on the property loan and stops funding the construction. Now what? Does the tenant spend capital to finish construction? What happens to the free rent period stated in the lease? Who maintains the building? Can the tenant terminate the lease—or are they stuck making rental payments on a building they can't occupy?

Risk assessment is key here to ensure the lease terms are honored and remain intact, that you will be assured you have a place of business should conditions shift, that your assets are protected, and that a smooth transition is assured after the ink dries on your contract. This applies to renewing a lease as well because market and financial conditions change. The bottom line: understand the landlord's ability to perform obligations of the lease and negotiate fail-safes to guarantee it.

When it comes to researching your options, it's simple, really. Once you figure out what you already know and learn what you need to know, then you'll know what you need to find out. When you follow that roadmap, you're on a smooth course to negotiate a great deal.

RECAP LAP
Research Market Options

Here's a guide for researching and monitoring market conditions and trends for creating your best position:

1. Scan the market to discover what current motivations and priorities are uppermost to landlords in your target market and microclimate. Research macroeconomic influences, regional market trends, commercial real estate availability, and price trends. If you are considering renewing your lease, this includes particular analysis of your current landlord's position.

2. Monitor regional lease rates and occupancy trends, as well as macro trends in commercial real estate. Know when conditions start to shift so you can act or delay to your company's benefit. Learn what moves signal that landlords are getting anxious about where the market is headed and maximize your window of opportunity.

3. Formulate your search strategy by developing a flexible plan that considers a broader search area, incorporates your microclimate, and analyzes space use options, including the possibility of dividing by use type. If you have special infrastructure needs, particularly in biotechnology, price out your proposed space plan to be sure the savings still pencil out.

4. Conduct due diligence to protect your business so you are confident of the landlord's ability to perform in accordance with the lease. Delve into their cash position

and financial stability to discern their priorities. Include investigation into the equity of the building and the owner's overall portfolio as well as cross-collateralization.

5. Build safeguards into your contract, including a subordination, non-disturbance and attornment agreement (SNDA), offset rights, and contingencies for building repair and maintenance. Plan for business continuity in the event the owner defaults on the loan or sells the property.

PLAN YOUR SPACE AND PRICE
YOUR CONSTRUCTION COSTS

THIS INFORMATION-DENSE CHAPTER is going to make
you look really smart.

When there's a lot to know about navigating the
minefield of tenant improvements, your efforts to command
a good working knowledge of the practical and financial
aspects involved will yield significant results for your company. Maximizing the return and efficiency of that expense
can't be overstated, nor how much your office environment
contributes to team spirit, pride, and productivity.

Defining Your True Needs

Early in the site selection process, the best starting place is an
overall needs assessment that delineates components of what

Prepared for: Name Goes Here			
	(Headcount)	Size	Sq. Ft.
Executive			
President & COO		16 x 15 = 240	0
CEO		16 x 14 = 224	0
CFO		14 x 14 = 196	0
General Counsel		12 x 12 = 144	0
Human Resources, Manager		12 x 12 = 144	0
Corporate Controller		15 x 15 = 225	0
Additional offices below as needed		10 x 10 = 100	0
		10 x 10 = 100	0
Space Allocation:			0
Departments			
Trading / Sales Teams		8 x 8 = 64	0
Systems Analysts		6 x 6 = 36	0
Labs/Manufacturing		8 x 10 = 80	0
Space Allocation:			0
Manufacturing Area (no circulation factor)			
Warehouse Area		50 x 100 = 5000	0
Biotech/Lab		50 x 50 = 2500	0
Space Allocation:			0
Shared Corporate Areas			
Main Reception		16 x 16 = 256	0
Lunch Room		16 x 16 = 256	0
Conference Rooms		18 x 22 = 396	0
Computer Room		18 x 20 = 360	0
Postage/Fax/Printers		14 x 10 = 140	0
Server Room		10 x 12 = 120	0
Space Allocation:			0
Circulation Between Personnel & Departments:	40%		
Common Area Factor Applied	15%		
Total Allocated Square Feet			0
Total Employees:	0		
Total Rentable Square Feet			0
Square Feet Per Employee			0

you will require in a new space. This is just as important when you prefer to renew your lease, are adding expanded space, or reconfiguring your current footprint. An existing conditions review will enable you to analyze what's working (or not) in your current space. Overlapping it with your projected staffing needs over the new lease term will allow you to develop a space analysis by use type.

This identifies the desired number of offices, workspaces, conference rooms, workstations, common areas, and specialty areas such as manufacturing, laboratory, warehousing, and shipping and receiving. It can be essential to fold in feedback from a cross-section of key stakeholders from various disciplines, generations, and demographics to make sure all voices are heard. With trends toward more work-at-home and office hoteling (elimination of assigned seating) options, this step can maximize efficiencies in your space plan.

Once drafted, this becomes your architectural program; it identifies everything you need as an organization to operate. This includes type, size, and number of offices, workstations, collaborative workspaces, conference rooms, reception, and specialty areas such as laboratory, warehouse, manufacturing, storage, and others. Do you require a copy/mail room? What about a kitchen or pantry? You can't evaluate a new space until you have a realistic estimation of your company's true space requirements.

Think of a test fit as a matchup between your needs assessment and your candidate site.

Next, an audit of furnishings and fixtures is in order. What will you retain and what will you replace? A general rule of thumb for new office furniture expenditures is twenty to twenty-five dollars per square foot. Remember to include furnishings and fixtures that are customized to your company's needs. Technology, including cabling and communications, as well as specialized equipment, should figure into your plan as well.

Once you've finalized your needs assessment, it's a great idea to engage an architect or designer early in the site selection process. They can help you identify things you may have overlooked or possibly miscalculated. An experienced professional can save you time and money down the road as they might spot deficiencies or surfeits that could limit your options and inflate your budget on an otherwise appealing site.

Developing Your Test Fit

So, you've found a candidate space and want to know if it will work for your business. This is when your architect or designer will create a *test fit*, a preliminary space plan that you can use to confirm all the requirements you have identified will work in a specific space. Think of it as a matchup between your needs assessment and your candidate site. Let's say your needs analysis has determined that you need twenty workstations, three conference rooms, a large reception area, a kitchen, a copy/mail room, and an area that contains about 45 percent biotech laboratory area. A test fit that includes fitting your furniture and equipment will assure you that the space you are considering will accommodate those needs.

This general layout of interior space will reveal how well your specific must-have components will functionally fit in a proposed space. If your site is already selected, a test fit can help you preflight your overall architectural program. Either way, remember to factor in growth projections from your business plan so you are assured that the space will continue to accommodate your workforce over the entire lease term.

A test fit really doesn't differ dramatically from a space plan, which is a more in-depth schematic of your interior space that technically lays out interior special areas, defines circulation patterns, and proposes placement of furniture and equipment. But it's a more comprehensive look at the space, beyond just whether your needs are satisfied within a space. It is a more descriptive analysis of how the space will look and feel.

When evaluating different buildings, understand that it is unlikely to occupy the exact square footage you may require. Each building has different load factors, floor plate locations to support heavy equipment, common areas, angles, and architectural features, all of which affect the efficiency of the space. Sure, the floor plan layout may look nice, but is the occupant paying for wasted space?

Generally, a motivated current or prospective landlord who wants to help you finalize your space selection will underwrite the development of your test fit. If not, it's still a high-value endeavor for your company to undertake because it gives you confidence that the vision you have for your new or reconfigured space works—and provides you with an optimal (and cost-efficient) workplace.

Costing Out Construction

All too often, hastily compiled ballpark estimates of tenant improvement (TI) costs turn out to be significantly lower than the real costs that materialize after architectural drawings and construction bids have been developed in detail. Should those early estimates get locked into the term sheet and lease agreement, your company is obligated for all of the overages. Consider bidding out the scope of work before dropping a TI figure into the term sheet. Find a number you're sure is realistic, or at least one you can live with, before signing a lease only to find out the TI allowance won't cover your TI costs.

When evaluating different buildings, understand that they are unlikely to match the exact square footage your plan requires. Each building has different inefficiencies. Case in point: A company requiring a 20,000-square-feet space paying rent of $2.60 per square foot per month will save $312,000 over a five-year lease term by leasing 10 percent less space. Before spending hours in the car with a real estate professional touring buildings, spend some time up front space planning using general occupancy standards. Then, analyze each building's floor plan and layout for efficiencies.

Financing Tenant Improvements

All things being equal, prudent financial managers would no doubt rather borrow funds at 7 percent than at 9 percent. So why, when it comes to the $200 billion financing market for tenant improvements, do risk managers and corporate real estate executives continue to allow landlords to earn outsize returns when alternative financing is available? The answer lies in debt capital markets, where pricing is tied to companies' debt issuance rates rather than landlords' cost of funds—and it is recognized as a practical way to finance TI costs. In addition, landlords are not banks and charge a higher interest rate due to the increased risk, compared to a traditional lender, when funding a TI allowance.

Historically, TIs have been funded by landlords, tenants, or in many instances, a combination of both. In addition to not being properly capitalized for this ancillary activity, landlords often fund TIs out of necessity in an effort to secure a tenant. During negotiations, tenants generally accept as many TI dollars as landlords offer.

If you decide to self-fund TI requirements, you may realize an immediate negative effect on the company's financial statement. The TI investments are reflected on the balance sheet as ownership of long-term, nonrevenue-producing assets with a corresponding increase in liabilities or cash reduction.

RECAP LAP
Plan Your Space And Price Your Construction Costs

Save valuable time and money by learning as much as you can about what to expect (and what to avoid) during the construction process of your renewal or relocation:

1. Conduct a comprehensive analysis of your needs, identifying components of everything you will require in a new space. Do it early in your process and overlay it with your projected staff needs over the new lease term.

2. Engage a design team and/or an architectural firm to develop a general layout of the interior space (test fit) to preflight your architectural project. This ensures the space you are considering (or reconfiguring) will accommodate your firm's specific, identified needs and plans for growth (while also confirming space efficiency and justifying square footage).

3. Bid out the scope of work before entering a figure into the term sheet. This is especially key because you will have to pay any overages after you have signed a not-to-exceed cost agreement for construction, or a TI allowance.

4. Research and explore TI funding options and alternatives so you are not lured into simply accepting a landlord's initial offer. Analyze your company's short- and long-term accounting goals and tax implications when structuring financing.

CREATE LEVERAGE THROUGH SIMULTANEOUS NEGOTIATIONS

NTI-APARTHEID ACTIVIST JOE Slovo once said, "You can't go to a negotiating table pointing a gun, but you've got to keep it over your shoulder."

In negotiations, leverage is something you use to articulate the strength of your argument to give you advantage. It bolsters your ability to influence and persuade, backing up your high-value proposition. Importantly, though, it's not about having an *overwhelming* advantage based on an ability to compel or coerce the other party. Overplaying your hand could risk resentment, damage the long-term relationship, or derail the deal. While leverage is a compelling advantage, fairness and equity also come into play. The goal is for both parties to feel victorious after closing the deal.

When you discover the lay of the land and work out how to create leverage, you're in the game. Whether you are renewing a lease or negotiating a new one, these are the forerunners to success: planning, discovering your options, understanding the tradeoffs, and minimizing risks.

Landlord Landmines

You are about to sign a major contract that has significant financial obligations for your company. Regardless of market influences, use caution and heed the Latin axiom *caveat emptor,* buyer beware. It is imperative to conduct your own due diligence to investigate the landlord's fiscal health to make sure they are on solid footing. Signing a multi-year lease in a highly leveraged building that is riding on thin ice could be a disaster.

First, do the necessary research or ask your advisor about the landlord's financial position and the capital structure for the prospective property. A landlord holding a troubled asset may downgrade the operation and defer maintenance of the building to conserve cash or they may refuse to honor tenant improvement commitments.

Landlord Leveraging

Alternatively, when a landlord is about to refinance the building and needs to drive up or stabilize long-term occupancy, you can definitely take advantage of the window of opportunity to gain significant leverage in the lease agreement. For example, published rental rates typically have negotiating room beyond free rent and other concessions motivated landlords may offer to secure a lessee. As always, the bottom line in lease negotiations is to first do your homework so you fully understand the motivations and limitations that define the landlord's position. Then leverage that information to your best advantage.

The Route To Renewing

No one likes to relocate a business when the lease expires unless it is absolutely necessary. Moving causes downtime, frustration, loss of income and time away from the core business. Most business owners feel this way, and landlords know it. It's a reality that lease renewals are going to come up every three, five, or seven years. This is your chance to see it as an opportunity to improve your deal and return value on the company's expense.

For companies who have remained in the same building and simply renewed the lease each time, the situation is a bit more tenuous. As a matter of (unfortunate) course, lease renewal rates are generally higher with fewer economic concessions than rates offered to new tenants leasing vacant space. So yes, oftentimes your loyalty as a repeat customer is practically null and void. Until you learn how landlords calculate real estate pricing, you won't be able to obtain a deal that is equal to the concessions a new tenant would receive.

> Until you learn how landlords calculate real estate pricing, you won't be able to obtain a deal that is equal to the concessions a new tenant would receive.

Let's take a look at how landlords evaluate their leverage when renewing a tenant's lease:

Statistics: Experience indicates that approximately 70 percent of all tenants renew or extend their lease upon expiration, sometimes even sooner. Chances are that the existing tenant will renew. With nearly three out of four tenants renewing, one would expect landlords to approach the process from a position of strength, confident they can easily get you to re-up at a higher rate. Tenants outside of the statistical norm who come primed with research, clarity, and a preformed strategy have a chance to capture the edge in negotiations.

Timeline Crunch: Those who start negotiating too close to expiration often have no choice but to renew the lease. Waiting too long to evaluate relocation alternatives always places the tenant at an extreme disadvantage. When relocation is the preferred alternative, a tenant with a typical requirement of 10,000 square feet needs to start planning twelve to fifteen months before the scheduled lease expiration. Companies need to allow sufficient time to compute internal space projections, evaluate market options, visit desired properties, negotiate proposals and lease documents, obtain city permits, and construct tenant improvements. Sure, you can do all of this in less time, but it creates stress and limits your options. Ultimately, when you are out of time, you are out of luck.

Telegraphing The Punch: Business owners understand the concept of leverage, yet ironically, most companies initiate lease renewal negotiations by informing their landlord that they are ready to renew. They have basically just signaled the landlord that there will be no competition from other buildings. When relocating, you naturally bring competition into play by weighing various buildings and locations to find the best deal. Why not follow this on renewals? Isn't it what you would you do if you wanted to relocate? Wouldn't you hire a real estate professional? The message is clear: *every time your lease comes up for renewal, treat it as an opportunity to consider relocation alternatives in earnest.*

Unrepresented: It's a little more common for companies to engage a tenant advisor when relocating than it is to seek professional expertise with a lease renewal. It is an expensive miscalculation. As previously discussed, landlords are unlikely to pass on commission savings to you because someone will be paid for their time. Most commonly if a tenant is unrepresented someone is paid both sides of the commission in one of these three scenarios, which are all three a conflicted dual agency: the landlord listing agent is paid both sides of the commission given they are the only broker involved; landlords often pay themselves both sides of the commission as they act as their own real estate brokerage firm; or, the landlord pays their property managers both sides of the commission. When you negotiate without tenant representation and without leverage, it's a safe bet that any savings are a small percentage of the higher rent they are likely to extract from you.

Knowledge: You are an expert in your field and are undoubtedly proficient at your business operations. Unless your business is real estate, consider the matchup in lease negotiations: you're sparring with someone who leases space all day long. Know your bailiwick: Hire an experienced real estate professional to level the playing field. They can help you achieve success in this effort so that you can get back to focusing on your core business; always collaborate with experienced real estate professionals who know the ins and outs of negotiating a commercial lease.

Bluffing: Your negotiating partner is sure to wonder, "Is this tenant truly in the market considering relocation and negotiating alternatives, or is all this talk just a smoke screen?" Never bluff. The stakes are too high. Maximizing your leverage in lease negotiations is part art, part science. There are significant upsides if you renew your lease or renegotiate your lease early; perhaps you can negotiate concessions that will allow you to gain an immediate rental rate reduction, lock in an existing low lease rate, add or decrease physical space, or receive early tenant improvement dollars. Other factors in your existing office space and building should be reviewed and evaluated, such as current building cash flow and future rental projections, tenant improvement costs to rebuild the space for a new tenant, downtime for vacancy, and new risk with a replacement tenant. Be comprehensive in considering all the angles that can help you make the most of every lease renewal.

> If your current landlord does not believe you are actively considering relocation, you've lost practically all leverage.

Know Your Position, Read Their Signals

When entering into negotiations for either a new or a renewing lease, it's key to know your goals. The best outcome is a win–win resolution where both parties feel good about the final agreement. While landlords want the highest price and tenants want the best deal, the two have to meet somewhere in the middle for a deal to close.

If you've done your homework, you have accurately assessed your company's space needs and analyzed your budget parameters. You have identified your must-haves and compared features, benefits, and drawbacks with each candidate property. You've studied the market, including your microclimate, and you've conducted the fieldwork of visiting candidate locations, even if relocating is not your first option. You've gathered some good intel on your landlord's position and motivations. Now, for each option, and preferably with the counsel of your tenant advisor, you calculate your *walk away* rate.

A good place to begin developing your proposition is to establish a general sense of how your current and prospective landlords are setting their rates. Typically, they calculate the cost of rent by multiplying the square footage of the space by the cost per square foot. The result is the annual cost, divided by twelve months, with possible additional costs for maintaining common areas or operating expenses, depending on your lease type. Be sure you ascertain all the associated property costs that are included in the rent calculation and who is responsible for which line items. These may include utilities, insurance, taxes, building security, and repairs. (Some of these may be nonnegotiable.)

It's important to introduce competition into the negotiation whether you are serious about the property or not, whether you really do intend to renew your lease or not. The object here is to convince your negotiating partner that they are competing for your business. It's worth underscoring: if your current landlord does not believe you are actively considering relocation, you've lost practically all leverage in the negotiation.

Bargaining Basics

Be Coy. Be measured and unhurried in your response to the landlord's first proposal. They may naturally conclude that you are shopping and comparing it with other lease alternatives.

Be Confident. Even when you're fairly sure you'd be happy with less, ask for more than you truly expect in your rental terms. They want your business and are likely to continue the conversation even if they think your initial offer is low (if it is stupid low, there will probably be no response). With your first counter, you've provided a starting point and set the framework for a win–win, so be aggressive. Sometimes, it is good negotiating practice to let the landlord respond to a request for proposal, thereby allowing the landlord to ante up first.

Be Calculating. Consider what your tenancy is worth to your current landlord. It's almost always more profitable for them to renew a lease than it is to find a new leaseholder. Real estate financial models include debt service, property taxes, operating costs, leasing commissions, legal fees, tenant improvement costs, CPA (certified public accountant) and other accounting fees, vacancy—the list goes on and on. Understand your landlord's renewal profits and the costs of their losing your tenancy compared to your relocation costs. If your business is like most, where it can cost the landlord four to five times more to secure a new tenant than to keep a current tenant, you've got one more chip on the negotiating table.

Landlords stand to suffer a loss in rent, additional expenses for upgrades, renovations, and marketing the space if you choose not to renew. Deduce the dollar value of keeping you as a tenant so you can use that information to win back a portion of it in your new agreement. When you renew your lease, tenant improvement dollars the landlord may be asked to fund for your renewal are typically far less than TI expenses for a replacement tenant; they incur less capital outlay for your renewal and also have zero down time. Use this knowledge to your advantage.

Be Circumspect. It's not just about the rent. It's a whole package of terms and conditions that all have value: improvements, renovations or upgrades, signage, parking, free use of conference or storage facilities, and so on. This is your chance to ask—when the landlord is competing for your business and amenable to add-ons that may sweeten the deal for you.

Be Confidential. Your negotiating parties must have limited access to your full position and true motivations. Whether you are aware of it or not, landlords may be friendly with someone else in your company, so be mindful to closely control information about your intents and purposes during the negotiation process.

Be Prepared To Move

If your current landlord approaches you about extending your unexpired lease, don't feel compelled to just jump on the offer. Remember, there are a lot of other landlords out there who are just as motivated to secure your lease commitment and drive up their occupancy levels, too. Many tenants think that moving is just too much trouble, but unless you have some very specialized facility requirements, the willingness to move can be a valuable negotiating advantage, and for most companies, is fully completed in one or two three-day weekends.

It's not unusual for landlords to offer moving allowances of five dollars per square foot to a new tenant.

While many perceive it is more cost effective to stay in place, there are cases where moving makes a lot more sense. Gaining a 20 percent discount on a new lease might be worth a little upheaval. Some of the possible benefits include free rent periods, increased improvement allowances, reimbursement of moving costs and basic IT infrastructure, not to mention if you are going to a newer space, the HVAC and interior finishes will be an added bonus and likely to stand the test of time much better than your older facility.

When you move, you don't usually go to a worse space, you go to an equal or better space which often includes newer or refurbed HVAC, new paint, and newer finishes. (Therefore, tenants typically won't need to budget money for refreshing its paint, carpet, lights, or deal with suspect HVAC for about three years.) Depending on the market, it's not unusual for landlords to offer moving allowances of five dollars per square foot. Free rent concessions may range from two weeks to two months per year of lease commitment depending on market conditions. On a five-year lease, this can work out to almost a full year or more of free rent. Even if you end up extending your existing lease, it's always a good idea to test the waters and see what alternatives are out there. It gives you confidence in the actual value of your tenancy and in your negotiating position.

Remember that your signature on a new lease document is extremely valuable to your existing landlord, as well as their competitors. With today's focus on driving up occupancy levels, a solid, creditworthy tenant enjoys even more negotiating power. As always, perform your due diligence to ensure that the landlord is in a strong enough position to follow through on their commitments. It's never beneficial to gain concessions that turn out to be empty promises. Once you're sure that the landlord is solid, use your negotiating strength to drive the best deal—one you never even thought possible. As always, the bottom line in lease negotiations is to do your homework to fully understand the motivations and limitations that define the landlord's position, then leverage that information to your best advantage.

RECAP LAP
Create Leverage Through Simultaneous Negotiations

There are definite steps and strategies to preparing your position and developing your proposition. Well before launching negotiations, tick off the boxes and draw up your game plan:

1. Research and evaluate potential landlord landmines and leverage points. Know with whom you are negotiating and conduct an honest appraisal of their position and motivations. Conduct due diligence to assess the financial stability of your negotiating partners and their ability to follow through on commitments.

2. Evaluate your worth as a renewing tenant and learn the landlord's perspective on your lease renewal negotiation. Gird yourself with a keen grasp of your potential vulnerabilities: shortcutting the time the process really takes, tipping your hand early, forgoing professional tenant representation, inadequate preparation, and bluffing.

3. Develop a thorough understanding of your goals. Research and develop an analysis of the strengths of your position and the motivations of your negotiating partners. Know your *walk away* rate.

4. Identify and introduce a viable competitor for your tenancy, even if you plan to renew your current lease. Conduct the same due diligence process for all parties and actively seek out and compare viable alternatives, weighing advantages and drawbacks of your choices.

Understand your own leverage points and those of your potential landlords.

5. Arm yourself with knowledge that will allow you to bargain intelligently. Be coy—measured and unhurried—confident, calculating, circumspect, and confidential. Prepare a valuation of the true worth your tenancy brings to your current landlord by calculating their cost of losing your business.

6. Commit to achieving a good deal for your company and resist taking the easy way out. Renewing without effort is sure to be quite costly, so actively seek alternatives—not just for negotiation purposes, but for the best outcome for your company. Be prepared to relocate if that's what it takes, as it can create positive returns for years to come.

7

NEGOTIATE THE TERM
SHEET AND LEASE

I F IT IS a match between underdogs and big dogs, odds are
with the big dogs, right? After all, they are well-trained
professionals with tons of experience. They are confident
and competent.

In contrast, underdogs are merely determined and daring.
They're not to be discounted, though, for there are thousands
of tales of triumphs of those who had the will and won the
way against the odds. (Ever hear the story of a hobbit named
Frodo Baggins?)

So now, as you prepare to enter lease negotiations, know
this: landlords negotiate leases on a regular basis. They are
well advised by many different consultants, including real
estate brokers, real estate attorneys, appraisers, lenders—you

name it. They have an experienced team advising them because this how they earn their income.

By hiring your own team of knowledgeable professionals, you can negotiate confidently; your real estate team will help pave your path to victory.

Convening Your Team

As discussed previously, the most important commitment toward obtaining a great outcome is to engage the services of a tenant representation broker along with other consultants, such as space planners, architects, construction managers, and real estate attorneys. Partner with people who know the ropes, who understand the market and the stratagems of the players. Your team of advisors will have access to valuable intel that will build and strengthen your bargaining position.

Simply by having professional representation, you are signaling that you are well resourced and expect competitive terms. Your current landlord will know that you are serious about considering relocation, and a potential landlord will know that you have access to current research on their building, their competition, and the market. A good broker will add value, not cost, and will bring inestimable expertise during negotiations. Having the right professional shoulder to shoulder with you throughout the process allows you to maximize results, avoid blind spots, save time, and reduce stress.

For optimal results, hire a broker—and the real estate firm the broker works for—who both specialize and exclusively represent commercial tenants to avoid the conflicts of interest. Landlords may sometimes try to negotiate with tenants directly, but it is advisable to have your expert present for all conversations with landlords, leasing agents, or building owners. Any direct discourse about the lease or discussion about terms of the deal conducted without your broker will greatly undermine your negotiation strategy.

Your attorney should work in concert with your tenant rep broker to review the lease terms, the lease, and any amendments. Make sure the two parties are acquainted and ready to work together to provide a united front in negotiations. You'll need to clarify expectations so that they stay in their lanes, however; attorneys shouldn't negotiate lease rates and terms and brokers shouldn't negotiate legal clauses. If you're fortunate enough to find a tenant rep broker with in-house counsel, you've got a specialist in commercial real estate legalities, and that's a home run.

Architects, space planners, interior designers, and contractors are other mission-critical team members who can provide the information and expertise you'll need to structure your position and develop your proposals.

Formulating Your Proposition

After you've completed your comprehensive needs assessment and conducted necessary research with the contributions of your team, it's time to match up your market analysis with a cost/benefit analysis of your options. Determining the value of your tenancy to both a current and potential landlord is an important component of your position, as is the research you've done to uncover the drivers behind their decision-making.

If you're considering lease renewal as an option, ascertain the value of your tenancy and the renewal profits the landlord is likely to chalk up for relatively little effort. The downtime of losing you as a tenant can take anywhere from a handful of months to several years, depending on leasehold size. The larger the space, the longer the potential stretch without rent. For a 10,000-square-foot space, for example, in my experience, the average downtime is nine to eighteen months. There are significant expenses the landlord will incur should they lose their tenant. A dozen or more months of lost rental income from the current tenant as well as incur tenant improvement costs that can range from twenty to several hundred dollars per square foot for the next tenant. They'll have to give away free rent; other concessions may be required. When they add it all up, it usually costs the landlord three to five times more to find a new tenant that it does for a tenant to find a new landlord.

You really can't expect to recapture all of that savings or the profit margin the landlord has built into the renewal. The goal is to achieve a deal that will yield a rate well below the market. One way to do that is to make sure there's an ethical negotiation process driven throughout the whole negotiation.

Lease Renewal Analysis (5 Year)

Replacement Tenant

Lease Assumptions

Rentable SF	10,000
Lease-Up Time (Mos.)	9
Construction Time (Mos.)	3
Term (Mos.)	60
Annual Rent Increase	3.0%
NPV Discount Rate	3.0%

Additional Leasing Costs

Tenant Improvement Costs (/RSF)	$35.00
Leasing Commissions	6.0%

Cash Flow Analysis

Period	Rent/SF	Annual Rent	Landlord Costs	Totals
Year 1	$2.00	$0	($410,244)	($410,244)
Year 2	$2.06	$240,000		$240,000
Year 3	$2.12	$247,200		$247,200
Year 4	$2.19	$254,616		$254,616
Year 5	$2.25	$262,254		$262,254
Total Rent				$593,826
Landlord Net Effective Rent/SF				$0.99
Average Rental Rate Over Term/SF				$2.12
NPV				$506,597

Lease Renewal

Lease Assumptions

Rentable SF	10,000
Lease-Up Time (Mos.)	0
Construction Time (Mos.)	0
Term (Mos.)	60
Annual Rent Increase	3.0%
NPV Discount Rate	3.0%

Additional Leasing Costs

Tenant Improvement Costs (RSF)	$12.00
Leasing Commissions	6.0%

Cash Flow Analysis

Period	Rent/SF	Annual Rent	Landlord Costs	Totals
Year 1	$1.19	$142,905	($165,581)	($22,676)
Year 2	$1.23	$147,325		$147,325
Year 3	$1.27	$151,881		$151,881
Year 4	$1.30	$156,438		$156,438
Year 5	$1.34	$161,131		$161,131
Total Rent				$594,100
Net Effective Rent (/RSF)				$0.99
Average Rental Rate Over Term				$1.27
NPV				$533,832

For illustration only. This model is not intended to represent renewal rental rates
but illustrate where an existing landlord breaks even on a renewal compared
to a new tenant factoring in downtime and tenant improvements.

Landlord Breakeven Analysis

Be scrupulous when calculating tenant improvement costs and take care not to underestimate what it will take to get the space customized to your needs and preferences.

If early estimates get locked into the term sheet and lease agreement, the tenant is stuck paying all of the overages. Bidding out the scope of work before locking in a TI figure will allow you to use your leverage before signing to establish a not-to-exceed TI cost that is as realistic as possible.

Incorporating Key Items

You want your lease to remain intact in the event the lender takes possession of the building.

Remember to obtain a subordination, non-disturbance and attornment agreement (SNDA) between your company and the lender of the property, if any. You'll want your lease to remain intact in the event the lender takes possession of the building. Another important lease clause, which is typically given to larger creditworthy tenants, calls for offset rights guaranteeing you the right to redirect rental payments to fix repairs should the landlord otherwise default.

Building In Exit Strategies

When signing a new lease, most companies focus on how the space will serve their needs over the lease term and spend little or no time considering the possibility that they might need to exit before the lease term is complete. Economic downturns clearly demonstrate the need to always have a backup plan. With commercial leases, the most common exit strategy is to sublease the space to someone else, though it can be challenging to find a sublease tenant whose needs are a perfect fit for your space. So, now is the time to plan ahead for this possibility. Think about how you might go about subdividing the space during the planning of your build-out, to sublease it faster in the future if needed. It may never happen, but if it does, a little foresight can make your exit strategy more realistic.

Your advisors can help you craft language that will provide for early termination, expansion, and contraction rights.

Auditing The HVAC Systems

One of the biggest potential cost factors that can pop up unexpectedly during the term of a lease is the need for expensive repairs to the HVAC systems. In triple-net leases and in some gross leases, the tenant can be solely responsible for such repairs. If nothing else, the headache is brutal, so investing in an HVAC system audit before signing is cheap insurance against this risk. If any issues come up, require the landlord to perform the appropriate services or repairs before signing the lease. Strong tenants sometimes demand that the landlord include a warranty against some HVAC failures. You may want to consider that older properties with outdated mechanical systems can often be harder to heat and cool, so the condition and proper functioning of HVAC systems are an important ongoing cost factor.

Ensuring Code Compliance

It's really important to watch out for any code violations or safety issues that need to be brought into compliance. Before signing a lease, it's worth proposing a blanket clause that the landlord will be solely responsible for the associated costs to remedy any such violations and issues. The space you're considering should be in good shape and look well maintained. In multi-tenant buildings pay special attention to the condition of shared infrastructure and support systems such as HVAC, water, power, and the like. Deferred maintenance can significantly increase your operating costs.

Skirting Lease Pitfalls

Here are some potentially buried skeletons in the lease term sheet you may want to uncover with your team:

- Lease start date (fixed versus floating)
- Building, environmental, and ADA (Americans with Disabilities Act) code compliance
- Early access
- TI overruns
- Who constructs the improvements, landlord or tenant?
- Lease type: NNN, gross, or modified gross
- Actual cost of after-hours HVAC
- Signage
- Holdover rent (125 to 150 percent)

Surrendering The Pawns

Beware of fighting over the small stuff. In any negotiation, there is an ongoing process of give and take. In order to get the best deal, you need to decide ahead of time which issues you can give on, and where you need to hold firm. Knowing the difference between your critical and noncritical factors and understanding the tradeoffs puts you in a much stronger position than if you just fight with the same intensity across the board. It's also a good practice to identify real economic and noneconomic issues and to quantify their relative effects so you know which ones are most important to your business. You may even want to throw in some red herrings at the beginning of the process so that you have something to relinquish later.

"Negotiating isn't about getting what you want or giving in to what the other party wants," says entrepreneur John Rampton. "It's not an 'either/or situation.' It's about having both parties walk away satisfied. Over the years, in both business and life, I've had to learn this hard lesson." Being well advised, prepared, and fair-minded should put you in the driver's seat to negotiating a great rate for your company.

RECAP LAP
Negotiate The Term Sheet And Lease

Now you're down to it: the place you've been heading toward, the time for which you've been preparing. It's "go time" to finalize and present your proposal and to test the mettle of your preparation for negotiation:

1. Convene a team of pros who will support and advise you throughout your negotiation process and beyond. Ideally, the captain of this team is a commercial real estate broker and real estate firm who specializes in tenant representation. Your attorney or a real estate attorney should work in concert with your tenant rep broker. You'll also need to bring on an architect or space planner, an interior designer, and a contractor if you're planning on any kind of tenant improvements or construction.

2. Conduct a cost/benefit analysis of your options. Calculate the value of your tenancy and the renewal profits the landlord is likely to gain so you know what is at stake for them and what it means for the strength of your own position. Understand the true costs of improvements at locations you're evaluating.

3. Find out what type of lease the landlords are offering and familiarize yourself with the risks and benefits of each type. Determine how much fixed expense versus financial risk your company can tolerate and prepare to counter offer terms that are in alignment with those goals and preferences.

4. Develop an exit strategy to plan ahead for the eventuality that you will require an early termination of your lease for a multitude of unanticipated reasons. Consider adding clauses for expansion and contraction rights as well.

5. Audit the HVAC systems to circumvent big-ticket repairs or replacement that can wreak havoc with your finances. Code compliance is another often overlooked and dicey area, so identify vulnerabilities and ask the landlord to pay for needed changes before you sign the lease.

6. Familiarize yourself with the more common lease pitfalls and consult with your team to review the lease and the term sheet closely to uncover any snares lurking there.

7. Fight for your kings and queens and be prepared to surrender a few pawns. When you negotiate from a position of strength and yet maintain an even-handed approach, it generally results in a win–win for both sides, assuring you of a mutually-rewarding association for years to come.

8

DESIGN AND BUILD

R. BUCKMINSTER FULLER was a twentieth century architect, systems theorist, author, designer, inventor, and futurist—although he preferred to be called a "comprehensive anticipatory design scientist." He is regarded as one of the most visionary thinkers of his time.

To this highly revered visionary, "a designer is an emerging synthesis of artist, inventor, mechanic, objective economist, and evolutionary strategist." Props to the design professionals who must now command these disciplines on your behalf. As you approach the design/build phase of your process, you may acquire newfound respect for the complexity and multidisciplinary blend of art and science intrinsic to transforming your workplace vision into bricks and mortar.

Your workplace communicates a lot about your company— reflecting image, atmosphere, operational efficiency, future growth, and even *esprit de corps*. In the process of designing your space and determining interior design and materials, you are building an environment for productivity, collaboration, comfort, and, if you're successful, innovation.

Site Vision

Unless yours is among the few companies not making any improvements to your space on a renewal or relocation, you'll likely need an architect or space planner to help you from start to finish. At the beginning, they will assist you in developing a comprehensive needs assessment and space programming plan to configure the kind of space you'll need, in both size and functionality. This allows you to determine what kind of square footage you're searching for in a new location or what adjustments will be required in your current space. By drawing up a test fit schematic, they'll help you determine if a candidate building you like will even work for your company.

It's worth underscoring here that when evaluating different buildings, few are likely to occupy the exact square footage required. Each building has different load factors (defined as the difference between the rentable square feet you pay for versus the usable square feet you occupy), floor plate locations for heavy equipment, common areas, angles, and architectural features. All of which affect the efficiency of the space. Sure, the layout may look nice, but will you be paying for wasted space? Remember that a company requiring 20,000 square feet at $2.50 per square foot per month will save in excess of $300,000 over a five-year lease term by leasing 10 percent less space.

When you've spent the extra time space programming, you'll be able to analyze each building's floor plan and layout for efficiencies. It's usually best to use general occupancy standards (which differ for office, biotech, manufacturing, or industrial space) and then overlay your business plan to account for anticipated staffing changes and workplace trends. Whether the candidate sites are nearly move-in ready or not, you'll want to figure out how your space requirements might be served by calculating the specific numbers of private offices, cubicles, meeting rooms, reception, and shared use areas. Add to this an additional 30 to 40 percent for circulation areas and an additional 15 to 20 percent for the building load factor for areas such as restrooms, corridors, and other common areas that are shared in a multi-tenant building. This will give you a realistic range for total rentable area required.

A more general ballpark is to plan for 175 to 200 square feet per employee (average density range) for general office space. Additional variances should be configured by use type for biotechnology, warehouse, manufacturing, or light industrial, which range from 250 to 350 square feet per employee for non-office use types. Those companies will need mixed-use locations, so space is split between office and specialty use in percentages; for example, 30 to 50 percent office and 50 to 70 percent for your unique use type (e.g., biotechnology, laboratory, manufacturing, warehouse, industrial). When determining if a space will work for your business, you can employ the most common method: guesswork. If you find that doesn't work too well in other aspects of administration, try the Goldilocks principle: find out for sure whether or not the space will fit just right. Also, make sure to take into account any hoteling spots, or work-from-home spots following COVID-19, which can reduce your office-only footprint by 25 percent or more with different workplace strategies post-COVID.

Design Matters

Next, you'll need an architect and project and construction manager on your team to help finalize design plans, cost out finishes, fixtures and furnishings, and coordinate construction. A good space plan is key to making sure your business is configured for efficiency and productivity, which can contribute to employee satisfaction as well. This includes features that consider employee well-being in the physical environment such as lighting, ergonomics, fresh air, privacy, and mobility. (Hint: Research shows that employees nearly always prefer a workplace with bright, natural light in a mostly open concept, subject to private office requirements, which are unique for every company. That type of workplace positively affects productivity and enhances morale, too.)

Building Out

The construction phase begins when you have finalized and fine-tuned the space plan, interior design, and architectural programs. Your architect will develop the construction documents, which basically serve as the construction blue-print. Also, be prepared to comply with state and local requirements for permitting. Meanwhile, your project and construction manager will obtain several bids from licensed *commercial contractors*, preferably those who specialize in your business sector to assess and compare costs from each contractor's bid.

Be precise about what you expect in terms of scope of work—are you planning cosmetic upgrades such as painting and replacing floors, or is more extensive demolition, reno-vation, or new construction required? Each space is unique, so research, vet, and select a construction partner with the experience, references, and communication skills that instill confidence. The right team will be licensed and totally con-versant in building codes, regulations, inspection, and per-mitting processes for your property. You'll be glad you did the legwork to find the right fit, because an unfavorable alli-ance can result in serious delays, budget overruns, or a work-place that doesn't function as intended.

Caution Ahead

Any number of unplanned potholes can send your construc-tion budget skidding off course. Comprehensive planning, closely coupled with appropriate cost estimating, should thwart major unexpected expenses. Even with the best plan-ning, there may yet be a few common oversights along the way. One of them is ADA compliance, so make sure your design team has it factored into your space plan or that the landlord will cover it and/or other compliance costs, not draw it from your tenant improvement allowance. While tenants normally pay for fabrication and installation of building top and monument signage, landlords usually fund suite and directory signage; these should be included in your negotiation. Tenants, except for banks with a small space in a large building, do not normally pay a monthly fee for building-top signage, provided the tenant leases a decent portion of the building (approximately 40 percent or more).

Be sure you understand the time it takes to effectively plan, price, and build your project. A typical twenty-four-month timeline is shown below, applying to a smaller-sized company needing 10,000 square feet (which may contract this timeline down to sixteen to eighteen months) to a business requiring well over 100,000 square feet (which requires a twenty-four-month timeline). The larger and more complex your space needs, the longer the process will take.

1. Needs assessment and architect planning: two months

2. Site visits to short-listed buildings: two months

3. Simultaneous negotiations with relocation and renewal option (if any): two to three months

4. Test fits finalized and budgets developed: one month

5. Execute Letter of Intent on relocation or renewal option: one month

6. Negotiate and execute lease (relocation or renewal): two months

7. Finalizing space programming and design development: two months

8. Finalizing construction documents and blueprints: one month

9. Permits and contractor bids: two to four months

10. Construction: four to nine months (pending space use and build-out needed—shorter time for office: four to six months; longer for biotech or manufacturing: six to nine months. Understand that construction may overlap with permitting by a couple of months.)

11. Fit-up new space, relocate or renew existing lease: last thirty to sixty days prior to natural lease expiration.

These typical duration estimates are noncontiguous, and some components occur simultaneously to the site selection and contract negotiation phases:

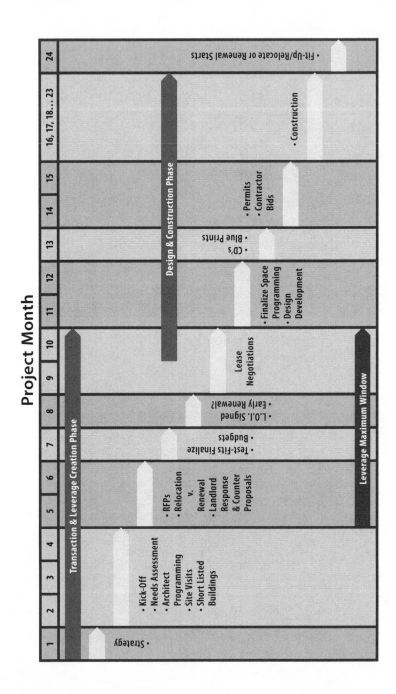

Project Progress

You should be in regular contact with your construction manager, who is ideally apprised of progress on a weekly basis via the construction meeting minutes, to ensure that the project schedule is on track. Don't hesitate to ask for photographs of the project's progression or for construction meeting minutes if you are unable to schedule regular walk-throughs. Assert your right to building inspection reports, schedule changes, and heads up on delays (actual or projected). Once construction is complete, a certificate of occupancy will signal that your space has been inspected and approved.

During the final walk-through with your construction manager, you'll review the punch list for your project, basically a checklist of the specific terms of the contractor agreement. Verify and mark each item as completed, but refrain from signing off until even minor issues are corrected.

New Signage

Building signage is a form of branding and advertising. It is necessary that retail businesses let customers know their location. For other types of businesses, signage is less crucial but can still provide multiple benefits, with name recognition leading the list. The perception of a company may be elevated because a dominant sign connotes stature. The more space a tenant is leasing, the higher up on the building their signage is likely to be—or even exclusive to the building itself.

Before signing a lease that provides signage rights, you'll want to prepare a visual of what you want the sign to look like, how big it will be, and on what facade of the building it should be placed. Your project and construction manager can aid with this process to ensure the proper sign vendor is in accordance with the landlord's sign program and compliant with all relevant city regulations. Typically, the tenant pays all of the costs associated with signage including design, installation, removal, and repairs to the building upon removal.

Your project should reflect the company's practical needs as well as its aspirations, employee welfare as well as its brand.

Sometimes, tenant improvement funds from the landlord can be reallocated to offset signage costs. Again, it's all in the negotiation. Building top signs can easily cost from $20,000 for low-rise buildings to $150,000 for signage on a downtown high-rise. Multiple colors, extensive lighting, and size can increase the costs significantly. Remember to check permitting regulations before getting too far along in the planning and design (and negotiation) of your signage.

Another consideration when evaluating a signage opportunity is ensuring that the removal of existing signage before new signage is installed will include any building repair necessary, and that it will not fall on your side of the ledger. The landlord should assume removal and building repair costs in preparation for your sign.

Your design/build project should reflect your company's practical needs as well as its aspirations, employee welfare as well as its brand. It's an amalgamation of practical considerations, from efficiency and productivity to health and safety to aesthetics and comfort. Aspire to a blend of form and function that would make architect Buckminster Fuller proud. "When I am working on a problem, I never think about beauty, but when I have finished, if the solution is not beautiful, I know it is wrong."

RECAP LAP
Design And Build

The vision is taking form now; the destination is in sight. Surround yourself with a team of pros who can bring it to fruition and coach you through the rough patches inherent in every project:

1. Understand the interplay between form and function as you approach the design/build process. An inspiring space is efficient, productive, and accommodating to those who use it. The best places serve people well, and practicality is paramount.

2. Partner with a project and construction manager, which a tenant representative brokerage company should have in-house, who will aid in hiring an architect or space planner early on to strategize, with a test fit, for maximum efficiency in determining square footage requirements. Otherwise, you'll pay for surplus square footage every month, which can be a painful tally when viewed over the entire lease term.

3. Plan for anticipated staffing changes and workplace trends. Match up your business plan for workforce expansion or contraction over the lease term period. Remember to include any projected use type changes in your ratio if office space is only a portion of your overall leasehold.

4. Trust your project and construction manager (who should be part of the team provided by your real estate broker or advisor firm) to help you think through and cost out finishes, fixtures, and furnishings. They'll also

help the architect or space planner coordinate and troubleshoot with the contractor.

5. Make sure your project and construction manager vets a licensed commercial contractor carefully. When accepting bids, be precise in your scope of work to ensure a no-surprises outcome. Find a team that is conversant in building codes, regulations, inspections, and permitting processes. As with design, this is a time when you'll want a good complement of form (communication and rapport) and function (experience and references).

6. Be rigorous in your project planning and cost estimating to preclude major potholes. Double-check with your broker, project and construction manager, and your design team for any planned fees or expenses you may have overlooked, such as permitting, ADA compliance, or things the landlord should be paying to avoid using your tenant improvement allowance.

7. Learn what to expect from your project timeline as mapped out by your project and construction manager and real estate team and what scheduling time frames are realistic for each step. Ideally, build in some wiggle room for the unexpected. The design/build functions are noncontiguous and are usually present in some respects throughout the entire timeline.

8. Know what you want and expect from your building signage and what portion you might propose the landlord underwrite. Check local regulations and the landlord's signage program before getting too far into the design process. Make sure you are not charged for removal of existing signage and attendant building repair.

9

ASSESS YOUR REAL ESTATE NEEDS AND COSTS ANNUALLY

A S HAPPY AS you may be with your terms and space you've created, there's just no such thing as a perfect lease. All leases are crafted by imperfect people and then are rarely referenced (by imperfect people) after they're signed. So when leases languish unheeded, clauses (and even a small word) can be overlooked, causing you exponential costs and time delays. Terms can be vague or misinterpreted. Keep in mind that market rates fluctuate. Astute companies who pay attention to their real estate market position, rental rates, and leasehold details, such as operating costs, ensure the best value and avert costly oversights and overages. Take heart, there are some steps you can take to eliminate the gremlins in your lease that may be poised to materialize.

Market Watch

Whether or not they're thinking of selling, most homeowners keep tabs on mortgage interest rates and regional housing market influences and fluctuations. It's part of protecting their investment and staying on par with prevailing rates. In the same vein, your company would be wise to monitor commercial real estate rental rates for the real estate type your company leases, whether it's biotech or laboratory space, office space, technology research and development space, or industrial space, to know where you stand relative to local market trends. So if you are paying four dollars per square foot and that's right at market rate, great. If market rate is five dollars a square foot, enjoy your low rent. Now, if market rate is three dollars a square foot and you're at five bucks, there is a potential jackpot of savings, provided early lease restructure requirements are met. What four requirements need to be met for an early lease restructure?

1. You must be more than 50 percent through your lease term.

2. You must have decent credit.

3. The building needs to work for you for the long term.

4. You must be above market in rent.

The name of the game is exchanging a lower rental rate because you are above market for giving the landlord an extra lease term. In other words, you tear up the lease twenty-four months before it expires, and the landlord drops your rent by a buck per square foot. However, when all four conditions are present, you have a really good chance of winning. But, if you only have two out of the four conditions, it becomes more problematic to pull off a restructure.

Rightsizing Audit

A good way to find hidden profits in your lease is by determining the space your company occupies is appropriate for your needs. Say you have 100 employees, and you currently lease 20,000 square feet. Though, what if the next year, you're down to sixty employees? Now you're paying for unused space. At that point, depending on your lease term, you have the option of subletting space or restructuring the lease to renew early, provided some of the criteria mentioned above are met. If you have less than 50 percent left on your lease term, you may be able to shed space and renegotiate a new term at a new rate. Basically, it is refinancing your lease rate and other economic terms. You're trading term for greater rental concessions from the landlord.

Annual Lease Reconciliation

Each year, typically in the spring, a landlord's accounting department or property management division performs a reconciliation of building operating expenses (such as property tax, building insurance, and maintenance) to true up or reconsolidate operating expense provisions from the prior calendar year's operating expense estimates for the building. Landlords have tenants of all rental sizes, though they like to keep the operating expense provisions within their leases all the same for easy accounting and to bill all tenants the same way. When different tenants, based on size, lease term, and creditworthiness, do negotiate different operating expense provisions, it changes what the landlord can charge tenants. To make it simple: smaller tenants obtain less favorable deals than large tenants. More buying power and more dollars are at stake for larger companies and the square footage they lease.

For example: say a building's operating expenses were fifty cents per square foot per month. The following year, the expenses jump to sixty cents per square foot per month. That's an increase in expenses of ten cents per square foot (20 percent). Now consider that one of the tenants, perhaps a company that occupies a full floor, has negotiated a provision that the landlord cannot pass through charges for a specific code compliance. Should the landlord then do a straight, across-the-board pass-through? Not without considering specific operating expense provisions negotiated in your lease, which prohibits a landlord from charging certain items to you. You could easily be overcharged simply from the landlord not checking your lease details on items it was agreed they would not charge you or pass through to you, hence, the reason to double-check that you are not charged as other tenants are and your exemptions are being honored.

I have seen accidental overcharges well into six figures, so it pays to investigate.

Just like reconciling your bank statement, it's prudent to review and reconcile your building operating expenses annually. Let's say your charges increase 1 to 4 percent. Possibly not a big deal because expenses fluctuate naturally, and that amount is probably not worth a deeper dive. What you're looking for are major red flags. If you suddenly discover a $20,000 pass-through you didn't expect, it's probably worth a call to your real estate advisor to check the lease to make sure it is allowable. To avoid leaving valuable savings on the table, have a real estate expert conduct a thorough examination of pass-through and other occupancy-related expenses.

Lease auditing is a real estate function, not an accounting issue. You need the knowledge and experience necessary to uncover and successfully recover charges that vary from real estate standards. Recoveries are definitely possible, though you may have a limited amount of time to notify your landlord of your intent to exercise your lease audit rights. I have seen accidental overcharges well into six figures, so it pays to investigate.

Statement Errors

Landlord operating expense statements may contain billing errors, though most times they are unintentional. The top five common errors are:

1. Tenant Reimbursements: Just two examples: If your lease is in a multi-tenant building, you could be paying for services directly and not part of common building services provided to all tenants. Benefits to other tenants should never be included in your operating expenses. Without a detailed review of the landlord's general ledger, it's unlikely you'll uncover these charges. Also, landlords sometimes forget to amortize capital replacement items over the proper useful life term.

2. Gross Up Errors: It is common for commercial leases to contain a provision allowing the landlord to bill operating expenses based on building occupancy of 95 or 100 percent. This adjustment, or *gross up*, is a complex calculation that may frequently contains errors. Without a detailed review of the landlord's gross up inputs and calculations, you probably won't discover these errors.

3. Capital Expenditures: Your lease may prohibit your landlord from passing through the costs associated with large repairs and replacement projects, or it may require the landlord to spread those costs over a number of years. Although a desktop audit may catch this error in the first year it occurs by comparing year-over-year expenses, without a detailed review of the landlord's general ledger, you are not likely to find incorrect operating expense charges that should be amortized equally in comparison years. Operating expense charges may be incurred at a relatively stable amount each year, which could mean they may increase over the average 3 to 5 percent per year.

4. Parking Garage And Other Non-Office Areas: Your lease may contain language excluding the costs associated with specialty areas of the building such as parking garages, retail areas, fitness centers, property management offices, and cafeterias. Since these costs are often combined with the expenses associated with the overall occupied portion of the building consisting of existing tenants, it is extremely easy for such costs to be erroneously overcharged and included in the building's overall operating expenses—and extremely difficult for you to identify in a desktop audit. This underscores the importance of negotiating the operating expense provision in your lease.

5. Ownership Expenses: Your lease should contain a provision requiring operating expenses passed through to be directly related to the operation, maintenance of the building, property tax, and building insurance (excluding your specific tenant improvements). Landlords often account for their expenditures on a building-by-building basis or on the entire project in the case of a multi-building commercial real estate property. They sometimes fail to separate costs that should not be borne by tenants or your company, depending on how you negotiated the operating expense provision. Examples include expenses associated with the preparation of space for tenancy, entertainment and tenant relations costs, ownership legal fees, and tax preparation fees. Without a detailed review of the landlord's general ledger, it's not possible to know of these overcharges.

Chosen Battles

Before retaining a lease auditor with real estate expertise, think about the risks and rewards. Will they damage your relationship with the landlord in the pursuit of all potential recoveries—even those that are insignificant and inflammatory? Make sure you instruct your advisor to "fight for the kings and queens and let the pawns go" to keep the relationship on good terms. It's paramount that your auditor's reputation in the industry drives credibility with landlords and provides an advantage in negotiations.

Lease Termination

How can you create more flexibility in your real estate holdings to adapt to changing business cycles? Terminate your lease. Well, that is, exercise the termination option if one exists. Of course, this must be included in negotiations during the writing of the letter of intent and before the lease is executed. As an example and rule of thumb, although everything is negotiable, this clause allows tenants to exit the lease at year three of a five-year lease term, at year five on a seven-year lease term, or at year seven on a ten-year lease term.

Not insignificantly, there is often an economic penalty tied to this termination right, which compensates the landlord for unamortized tenant improvement allowance dollars, brokerage commissions, legal and other consultant fees, unamortized free rent, and rent for a period equivalent to some landlord downtime, generally three to six months, to secure a replacement tenant. All of these points are negotiable, however, depending mostly on market conditions and the tenant improvement allowance funds the building owner has fronted. While termination options can be difficult to achieve (and some landlords just won't grant these rights), they can trigger agility if your business changes or the market softens significantly. Those options provide key flexibility for companies who are expanding, contracting, or evolving through mergers and acquisitions.

Leases are like people: none are perfect. They also need care and attention from time to time. Really, just a bit of oversight to be sure they are achieving their potential and sometimes, gentle correction if they get a little off course.

RECAP LAP
Assess Your Real Estate Needs
And Costs Annually:

Checking in on one of your major expenses should be a fairly regular feature of your company's to-do list. Negotiate a great lease and then make sure it's delivering that great value year after year:

1. Keep abreast of current commercial real estate markets to anticipate changes that may work for or against you. Learn about trends and influences that affect your lease rate and what you can do to correct it, if necessary.

2. Check periodically to confirm that your company's space is appropriate for your needs and not underutilized. You can find hidden profits by subletting unused space or renegotiating a new lease term and shedding space early.

3. Conduct an annual reconciliation of operating expenses by comparing statements from previous years. Flag any significant aberrant charges and consult your real estate advisor and the lease agreement. If you are alarmed enough to conduct a formal audit, retain a professional who specializes in commercial leases.

4. Watch out for errors in operating expense statements and understand the areas where the most common errors occur: tenant reimbursements, gross up errors, capital expenditures, maintenance such as HVAC charges and roof repairs, parking and non-tenant occupied areas, and other landlord expenses. While an annual desktop audit

may not uncover all of these, it can provide clues to lead you in the right direction when deciding to investigate further.

5. Determine if it's in your company's best interest to exercise the pre-agreed lease terms for early termination. Weigh the costs and benefits, as there may be unsupportable costs and conditions of so doing. When it does work out, it can provide agility and flexibility during expansion, contraction, or evolution through mergers and acquisitions.

10

INTO THE FUTURE

OES THE TREND toward more people working at home spell the end of the *edifice complex*?

Most companies will probably always need a centralized workplace. However, it may look different in the future; some may elect to downsize, trade out traditional office space for more hoteling spaces, or divide premises into more geographic locations. Some can't wait to get back to work and are looking at expanding given their recent growth. It is all over the map. Yet while biotech or laboratory space, industrial, and R&D real estate remain in high demand, office space is still lagging across the board in most markets. And if it's not lagging, it's getting converted into biotech or other space use.

Many industries will always mandate commercial space such as workplaces that require specific operating systems and infrastructure. Think of companies in manufacturing, biotechnology, distribution, and clinical services. There's probably a bigger emphasis on workplace usability and space efficiency than ever before and that should continue well into the future, so innovation and new possibilities will undoubtedly emerge to address evolving demands.

Sustaining Market Savvy

In the future, it will be more important than ever to stay abreast of market trends in rates, concessions, and landlord motivations and positions. It's a good idea to keep tabs on both macro and micro levels—that is, influences developing in the regional market, your microclimate, your building, and with your landlord. Tuning in will assure that you can avert downturns and seize opportunities. Checking in annually with the real estate pro who worked on your current deal may shortcut your research; they are in the field every day and have the proverbial ear to the ground. Whether you're looking ahead to an expected lease renewal or relocation, begin building your negotiation strategy well ahead of your need to employ it. Conversance with your market and your company's real estate position may allow you to seize opportunities or avert major damage to your budget. By attending to financial and legal implications of your current leasehold while also planning and forecasting the next deal, you'll be safeguarding the company's bottom line.

Decoding The Deal

Why cram for the exam? Good preparation and research can help you sustain the clarity you found in the real estate process last time around. Keep noting what's working well with your company's space programming and what might be heading for a course correction, especially if workplace needs are expanding, contracting, or shifting. Try thinking of this as a bank of leverage points fortifying your future deal. You may just become so confident that you'll look forward to your test—negotiating a new deal.

Streamlining The Process

You may be tempted to reason that, having learned what to expect, the process of your next lease will be straightforward and less complicated. Good luck with that. Flippancy aside, it may well be that you will have a hiccup-free process with total agreement in negotiations and perfect realization of tenant improvements. But to expect the unexpected may be a better bet. In commercial real estate, no two spaces are the same, no two clients have identical needs, no two landlords have the same motivations, and no two workplace requirements are identical. Every deal is unique.

You've now learned how to research and analyze your options and when it might be a good move to renew your lease, or even to restructure your lease early. You've identified landmines and red flags so your risk assessment should protect your assets and ensure a smooth transition. You now understand how to assess the landlord's ability to perform obligations of your lease and how to negotiate fail-safes to guarantee it. The mysteries of space planning, test fits, costing out construction, and financing tenant improvements should be less opaque now; the tool chest you'll need to confidently enter simultaneous negotiations will be well honed. You'll also have support and reinforcement from your real estate team, who will equip you with valuable information and insight to help you negotiate the term sheet and the lease. Best of all, they'll be there to bring your vision to life during the home stretch—the design and build stage.

Forecasting Tomorrow

Commercial real estate futurists didn't foresee COVID-19 and its overnight effects on the workplace—or the roughly 30 percent downsizing of pure office space use that resulted from it. For research and development, biotechnology, and warehousing companies, demand rapidly accelerated during that period throughout most areas of the United States. Biotechnology commercial real estate rental rates are at an all-time high in nearly every set market in the country. So to predict future markets, crystal balls become quite cloudy at times. Forecasts fluctuate dramatically by microclimate, depending on total square feet required as well as by use type (office, industrial, laboratory, flex). While it can be difficult to project commercial real estate trends, there are inferences to be drawn from today's landscape.

Companies requiring 30,000 to 50,000 square feet and greater will probably always have far fewer options in the market than ones looking for 5,000 or 10,000 square feet, though competition for smaller prime locations and rental rates may be more, too. Competition is high when availability is low, posing a special challenge for big tenants.

The trend toward an open office layout with fewer dedicated private offices will continue for some companies that are pure office tenants; however, many are going back to a little more dense private office workspace compared to nearly 90 percent workstations. Biotech companies, where private offices are more prevalent given their special requirements, will likely always have a demand for a greater private office percentage. There is a continued shift to include more small meeting rooms that double as hoteling offices for increasing numbers of employees working from home part of the time.

Working From Home

There are research studies to support both sides of the conversation about whether employees who work offsite are more or less productive, more or less engaged, more or less satisfied. At the end of the day, it's about adaptability and figuring out what works best for your workforce and for your company. Virtual meetings have become commonplace, and it's probable that some degree of remote working will be a long-term part of nearly all workplace strategies. Consider the benefits of reduced operating expenses and the ability to offer employees more flexibility and autonomy in their work environment. Expect more technology and design adaptations to better accommodate virtual interaction.

Putting People First

Physical proximity can reinforce company culture, foster communication and collaboration, and fuel teamwork. Some degree of in-person contact will always be ideal, and most companies will need to strike a balance between their real-world physical workplaces and virtual representations of such. People need a place to come together to build relationships, connect with others who understand their work, and develop their careers.

Leaders want to bring teams together to share their vision, incite inspiration, and affirm commitment to their goals. There may be a move toward achieving a better balance between distance and connectivity among workers and their colleagues, so the landscape is ripe for creative innovations to emerge, especially as new technologies unfold that allow us to entirely reimagine the workplace. Merging the practical with a dash of prowess, dare to consider the workplace with innovations and technologies that achieve your aspirational ideals for productivity, partnership, and profit.

RECAP LAP
Into The Future:

While commercial spaces of the future may look a bit different, most companies will require specific operating systems and infrastructure that necessitate centralized physical locations. Commercial real estate markets and microclimates may expand or contract (or both, simultaneously) depending on external factors and companies' mission-critical objectives:

1. Note that while the *edifice complex* of yesterday may be scaled back a bit, it's definitely here to stay in some shape or form for most companies. There will be a continued emphasis on workplace usability and space efficiency to economize and leverage return on this major expense.

2. Sustain attention on your real estate position throughout the lease term to monitor market volatility. Watchful executives will be able to seize opportunities and avert loss by taking action during market corrections and unforeseen circumstances (such as the pandemic).

3. Observe what's working well for your company's space programming and what needs to be reimagined (sooner or later), especially if your workforce is expanding, contracting, or shifting. Use the knowledge you've gained about the process to keep ahead of trends—and your company's evolving needs.

4. Understand the competition you'll have for limited availability if you're looking for locations of 30,000 to 50,000

square feet or more. Know that there are vastly more options in the 5,000 to 10,000-square-feet ranges, though there is also more demand, influencing rental rates and competition for desirable locations.

5. Figure out what works best for your workforce and for your company when it comes to finding the right balance of work-from-home and on-site employees. Plan work-place adjustments to provide spaces for employees who need quiet, privacy, or small-group confabs.

6. Remember that communal physical space can foster company culture, communication, collaboration, and *esprit de corps*; your company's physical location can provide unity of purpose, people, and projects.

7. Envision how your company might move toward a cohesive equilibrium between distance and connectivity among team members and their colleagues. Think about how physical space contributes to that goal. Reimagine the workplace with innovations and technologies that achieve your aspirational ideals of productivity, partnership, and profit.

APPENDIX

ACKNOWLEDGMENTS

I would like to thank my awesome wife and best friend Frederica. Her support and love has been tremendous. I would also like to thank my daughter Kiley and my son Jake for all of the great times we had in the early days and now watching them grow up and become mature young adults. I am proud.

A big thank you to Jason and Shay Hughes, and the Hughes family, for all of their love and support, friendship, partnership, and advice over the years.

Last, thank you to David Marino for his mentorship, energy, partnership, and friendship. It's been a great journey.

ABOUT THE AUTHOR

SCOT GINSBURG IS a licensed tenant representation commercial real estate broker who helps companies, and their executives create win–win leaseholds by taking the mystery out of landlord and commercial lease negotiations. For over two decades, it has been his passion to exclusively represent tenants when assessing space needs, evaluating, and locating the right facility, negotiating commercial leases for new space including tenant improvements, restructuring leases early to enhance savings, and negotiating lease renewals (given lease renewals are one of the highest profit margin transactions for most landlords). He draws upon his extensive multidisciplinary experience in representing nearly 2,000 tenants, providing resources and creativity to help them maximize value and deliver profits right to the bottom line. As a result of his deft leasehold negotiations, he has empowered clients to realize substantial savings, translating into millions of dollars saved in rent and other real estate lease costs, and dodging pitfalls.

Combined with a dedication to helping people, Scot's knowledge of the technical details of facility infrastructures, real estate financing, venture funding, burn rates, and lease contracts afford his clients a collaborative partnership based on trust. As senior vice president for the San Diego office of Hughes Marino, the nation's most highly regarded tenant representation firm, he offers unmatched expertise and deep operational support to clients. Scot's clients, namely those in San Diego, Orange County, Los Angeles, San Francisco Bay, and other metro areas of the country, benefit from the firm's in-house real estate counsel, construction and project management, portfolio lease administration and audits, workspace planning, and design.

On a personal note, Scot's lifelong fascination with car racing has progressed from racing karts to high performance cars to competitive race cars. He also enjoys managing his small-apartment investment properties and rental homes along with his wife, Frederica. Scot and Frederica also cofounded ScratchMyBelly.org to save animals from high kill shelters all over the USA and Mexico.

Scot can be reached at scot.ginsburg@hughesmarino.com or you can call him at 858.344.5000. Learn more about his capabilities and services at his LinkedIn page: https://www.linkedin.com/in/scotginsburg.

Made in the USA
Monee, IL
09 November 2023